THE WHITE KIKUYU
Louis S.B. Leakey

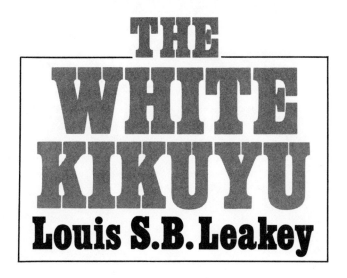

THE WHITE KIKUYU

Louis S.B. Leakey

BY ANNE MALATESTA
AND RONALD FRIEDLAND

McGRAW-HILL BOOK COMPANY

NEW YORK · ST. LOUIS · SAN FRANCISCO ·
AUCKLAND · BOGOTÁ · DÜSSELDORF ·
JOHANNESBURG · LONDON · MADRID · MEXICO ·
MONTREAL · NEW DELHI · PANAMA · PARIS · SÃO
PAULO · SINGAPORE · SYDNEY · TOKYO ·
TORONTO

Photographs appearing in photo section courtesy of The National
Geographic Society.

Library of Congress Cataloging in Publication Data

Malatesta, Anne.
    The white Kikuyu, Louis S. B. Leakey.

    SUMMARY: A biography of the anthropologist who made
important discoveries in eastern Africa concerning man's origins.
    1. Leakey, Louis Seymour Bazett, 1903–1972—Juvenile litera-
ture. 2. Anthropologists—Great Britain—Juvenile literature.
[1. Leakey, Louis Seymour Bazett, 1903–1972. 2. Anthro-
pologists] I. Freidland, Ronald, 1937– joint author. II. Title.
GN21.L37M34   570'.92'4[B]   77-78765
ISBN 0-07-039750-3

1234567890 MUBP 78321098

To Dan and Joan Marovich

Acknowledgments

Gratitude is expressed to Dr. Glynn Ll. Isaac and Mrs. Barbara Isaac, Department of Anthropology, University of California, for their helpful comments and reviews during the preparation of this book.

Gratitude is also expressed to the following publishers for permission to quote from their works:

California Monthly

National Geographic

Harper & Row, Inc.—*Adam's Ancestors:* The Evolution of Man & His Culture by Louis S. B. Leakey, 1953.

Houghton Mifflin, Co.—*In the Shadow of Man:* by Jane and Hugo van Lawick-Goodall, 1971.

David McKay Co., Inc.—*Digging Up Adam:* The Story of Louis S. B. Leakey by Mina Mulvey, 1964.

Schenkman Publishing Co.—*White African:* An Early Autobiography by Louis S. B. Leakey, 1966.

————*Adam or Ape:* A Sourcebook of Discoveries About Early Man, edited by Louis S. B. Leakey and Jack and Stephanie Prost, 1971.

Contents

Contents

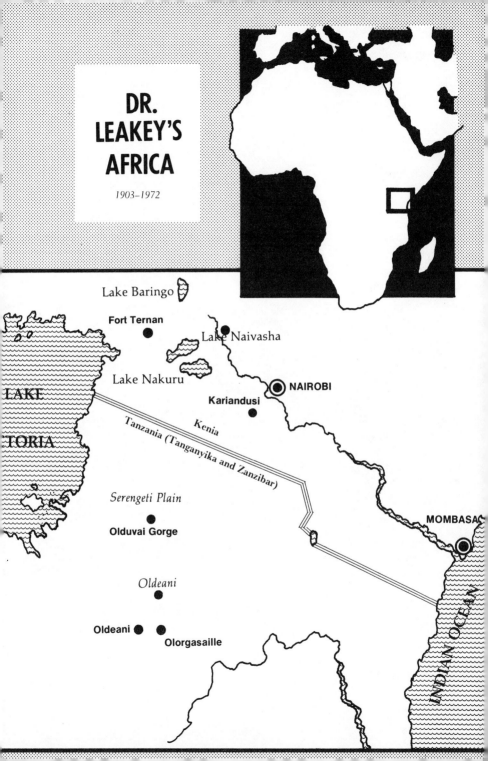

DR. LEAKEY'S AFRICA

1903–1972

Lake Baringo

Fort Ternan

Lake Naivasha

Lake Nakuru

NAIROBI

Kariandusi

LAKE

TORIA

Tanzania (Tanganyika and Zanzibar)

Kenia

Serengeti Plain

Olduvai Gorge

Oldeani

Oldeani

Olorgasaille

MOMBASA

INDIAN OCEAN

Birth of
a White Kikuyu

On August 7, 1903, a group of Kikuyu warriors wearing short calico cloaks and armlets of brass waited outside a small brush hut in Kabete, East Africa. Inside, a local woman boiled water over a crude brazier of charcoal, filling the mud-walled shack with acrid smoke. Then it began to rain. A sudden tropical storm beat against the thatched roof, and water deluged the people huddled below. Tribesmen hurriedly climbed the rounded roof to spread tarpaulins, but it didn't help. The cool night air blew through the wooden shutters, and puddles spread across the rough dirt floor.

The men stood silently in the downpour, a respectful distance from a tribal elder clad in a cloak of hyrax (rock rabbit) skin and holding a ceremonial spear decorated with ostrich feathers. It was a symbol of the importance of the moment. Then suddenly there was a cry from the hut. And then another. A white man hurried through the rain, pulled open the door, and went inside. When she saw him the local woman held up a tiny squalling infant, and he took it in his arms. It was his firstborn son, Louis Seymour Bazett Leakey. Outside, in the darkness, the elder nodded his blessing. The signs were propitious. Although

1

he could not know it, this child born on such a tumultuous night would bring about a storm of his own. In time he would shatter people's estimate of the dim past and reveal the earliest origins of the human race.

Louis Leakey was born in Africa because his British mother and father had come to bring the word of God to tribes such as the Kikuyu. In 1891 the young Mary Bazett, barely twenty, had been living in Reading, a suburb of London. She longed for something more exciting than the humdrum life of Victorian England. Her imagination had been stirred by accounts of David Livingstone, who had spread the word of God in Africa in an attempt to lead the black population toward a nobler way of life than the one under the Arab slave traders.

Her chance came when she heard that the Church Missionary Society needed volunteers to spread the gospel in British East Africa. Her enthusiasm infected her sisters, and when they decided to accompany her, the Bazett parents became worried because of the dangers of life in Africa, the tropical diseases, the wild animals, and the hostile people. In an attempt to discourage their daughters they even warned of savage tribes. They were certain their children would never return.

Nothing the British Army colonel and his wife could say or do would discourage the determined sisters. Their only consolation was that the girls would be doing useful work. Knowing there was no way to stop them, the parents watched their daughters board a steamer bound for the British Crown Colony of Kenya. They waved a reluctant good-bye.

Before reaching the shores of Mombasa, Kenya, the strong-willed Englishwomen had to undergo the strenuous sea voyage. They slept on deck, ate what simple food was provided, and endured the storm-tossed days and nights on the open Atlantic.

The steamer took turns sailing with favorable winds or chugging under power down the west coast of Africa and up the Indian Ocean. After months it finally rounded the Cape of Good Hope, and the Bazett sisters, utterly exhausted, offered a prayer of thanks at having reached the southernmost tip of the vast continent. Ahead was the last lap of the trip into the Indian Ocean before steaming into the old harbor of Mombasa. In his autobiography, *The White African,* Louis Leakey comments on his mother's arrival in the primitive Arab-Swahili village: "So far as I know, they were the first white women without husbands to set foot in that coral isle."

While her sisters traveled farther inland, Mary Bazett chose to remain in the exotic Arab seaport, which had been visited almost four hundred years before by Vasco da Gama. Her life there, however, was considerably different from that of the great Portuguese explorer. Da Gama had found his stay to be like a tale out of the *Arabian Nights.* He had been royally entertained by a king, resplendent in a green satin robe as he sat in a bronze chair with soft, embroidered cushions. Beneath a canopy of crimson silk, da Gama had listened to music from trumpets of richly carved ivory.

Mary Bazett did not enjoy such comforts. She lived austerely, trying to reach the members of the Swahili tribes working on the plantations. She learned to speak Kiswahili in order to communicate with these coastal people. She found that over a period of many years Hamitic peoples from Ethiopia and lower Egypt had moved into the area. They intermarried with the Bantu people that were there before them. Later many Arabs moved into the area.

3

In addition to her studies, and her attempt to gain the goodwill of the people, she also taught English to some of the Moslem women of the island. The heavily veiled women, kept isolated behind the stucco walls and wrought iron grilles, watched the fair-skinned English girl with fascination. Her freedom and energy surprised them. They appreciated her visits as much as the strange language she taught them.

With her duties over for the day, Mary was free to walk along the Fort Jesus Road and peer into the windows of the *dukas,* the "shops." In the showcases were richly carved ivory rhinos, woven baskets, silks and satins, spices and jewels, and implements hammered from brass and copper. She particularly liked mingling with all types of people on the crowded avenue, from the Giriama tribesmen with their elaborate bracelets of elephant hair to the fierce-looking bearded Sikhs in their colorful turbans.

But after three years of a hard yet rewarding life in this colorful meeting place of Africa and the Orient, Mary had to return to England. She had, as her parents feared, contracted a tropical disease. Arriving weak and exhausted after a long sea voyage, she was told by her English doctor: "If you know what is good for you, you will forget all about Africa." He didn't know his patient very well. This determined, stubborn young lady did know what was good for her. And that was a return to East Africa as soon as possible.

She had to wait a few years before going back, however. And then she was accompanied by a family. In 1899 she married Harry Leakey, a handsome, young curate serving in a London parish. He was also preparing for the life of a missionary in Africa. After the couple had two daughters they decided it was time to go. An appeal for volunteers had come from the church society. Harry hesitated, but his wife was adamant. Mary Leakey brushed up on her Swahili, packed the family belongings, and prepared the family for the trip.

Her husband insisted on going ahead alone to get things ready. He left England in December 1901, to establish a mission at Kabete and to take over a thatched hut that had belonged to the previous minister. A few months later he met his wife and daughters in a crude oxcart at the railroad station in Nairobi, a town that took its name from the Swahili word for "sweet water." Nairobi, with its sheet iron bungalows, shanty stalls, and brush huts was eight miles from Kabete.

Wearing a large mushroom hat that shaded her delicate skin from the blazing sun, Mary Leakey climbed down from the wooden railway coach and joined her husband. The fifteen-mile-an-hour pace of the team of oxen gave her ample time to see the *shambas,* the "fields," planted with potatoes, sugar, bananas, and maize. A dark tribal beauty, with her baby tied to her back as she worked in the coffee fields, stopped to watch this unfamiliar group of Europeans crowded into the rough cart. As she waved and called out, *"Jambo, Mem Bibi"* Mary Leakey knew she was home.

The hut she entered a few hours later was to be the place where her first son would be born several months later. The baby arrived prematurely, and the eager Kikuyu tribesmen would have to wait for their first glimpse of the child. Finally he was strong enough for his formal introduction, and his nurse Miss Oakes, wheeled his carriage out into the sun. The Kikuyus, bodies painted with ochre, solemnly filed past the infant. Their ceremony was partly respect and partly curiosity. They had never seen a white baby before.

The tribal elder had warned his tribesmen of their alternatives in greeting the newborn child. He had told them, "Now you can bewitch the new baby and cast an evil eye on him. Or you can put your seal of trust in him." Dressed in his full religious regalia the old man went up to the carriage. The other tribesmen waited anxiously to see what he would do.

He paused at the pram and regarded the baby carefully. Then he leaned forward and forcefully spat on it. The nurse pulled back in shock, but she had misinterpreted the gesture. It was the friendliest action he could perform. He had offered his brotherly love by giving something of himself. It showed a deeply felt devotion to a child the tribe would come to accept as a white Kikuyu. To them Louis was a black baby with a white face.

As Dr. Leakey later explained it, "The Kikuyu believed that the part of another person, a fingernail, a lock of his hair, or even his spittle, gave one the power to work deadly magic against him. By the same token the elders were putting their lives in my hands." He grinned as he added, "I was the best-washed baby in East Africa."

Louis was a lively child, and Kabete was a beautiful and endlessly interesting place for such a bright, curious boy. The church mission and school covered sixteen lush green acres. Gardens and huts were provided for the local people. Rich fields spreading beyond the compound were surrounded by the vast, empty bush country, which was as primitive and wild as in prehistoric times.

The sturdy four year old had very few white children to play with. The scattered farms of the English settlers were far apart. Only once in a great while would Louis see an Englishwoman dressed in a flowing ankle-length dress. Tightly laced in her European costume, the visitor to the Kabete mission carried a parasol to shield her face from the broiling sun. Unlike the Leakeys, the other foreigners had made no attempt to adapt to the ways and customs of their new land.

More familiar were the Masai women who lived several miles from Kabete. Their bare shaved heads gleamed in the sun. They wore huge collars of strung beads and coiled wire. Flung over their shoulders were rust-colored blankets, and tied to their backs were their babies. Louis watched these women build the family huts of brush and dried cow dung. Their warrior husbands, whose bodies were bright with red ochre, preferred hunting to the chores at home.

The Masai were a proud, handsome people with the sharp, bold features of the faces engraved on the ancient tombs of Egypt. This tribe is said to have come down from Northern Africa by way of the Great Rift, a gigantic crack in the earth's crust half the length of Africa. As long as people can recall, this nomadic tribe has been on the move seeking grass for their large herds of cattle.

Unlike them, the Kikuyu were farmers. These intelligent, hard-working people loved their fertile highland farms with a fierce devotion. While the husbands of the families hunted *nyama,* "meat," their wives in bright bandanas would plant food in the dark rich earth with digging sticks. Usually there was a child in their laps and another on the way. Pregnant and with a sixty-pound sack of potatoes on their backs, they would think nothing of walking the eight long miles to Nairobi for supplies. Louis came to have sympathy and respect for their endurance and dedication to their families.

The work of the Leakeys was sometimes tiring and frustrating, and they occasionally needed a leave of absence from their missionary duties in Kenya. In 1904 when Louis was a year and a half old, the family left Africa for what would be the first of many visits to Reading. They invited Stefano, a Kikuyu youth, to go with them so that they wouldn't lose their facility in the difficult language it had taken them so long to master.

A year and a half later, they returned from England to the new stone bungalow that had replaced the crumbling mud and thatch hut. The bungalow had a corrugated iron roof and wood ceiling. It was in that year of 1907 that another child was greeted by the Kikuyu, Louis's younger brother Douglas. This time there was room in the house for a young governess to tutor and look after the four children. The Leakeys recruited a woman, Miss Laing, from South Africa who must have had serious second thoughts when she arrived.

Because of pressing duties at the church mission, Harry Leakey had been unable to meet her in Nairobi. When Miss Laing alighted from the train she found four Kikuyu warriors in tribal dress waiting for her with a swing hammock. She was terrified by the lean, muscular men armed with spears and swords. After the jolting, panic-stricken ride to Kabete she jumped out of the hammock and ran into the house, amazed to find herself still alive. As it was to turn out, she was only the first of a long succession of governesses who could not endure the life that the Leakey family preferred to any other.

In addition to the lessons in reading and arithmetic, Louis and his brother and sisters learned more about the Kikuyu language and the customs of their tribal friends. Kikuyu was spoken as frequently in the house as English, and Mariamu, a local woman, often lulled the children to sleep with African songs and folktales. Mariamu told legends about every bird and beast and at the same time passed on the lessons of wisdom she herself had learned. One that Louis was to remember was a story about how the lowly hare outwitted the powerful lion. It illustrated that being wise was greatly superior to being strong.

The young white Kikuyu also participated in the daily life of the neighboring tribes. He often visited the *thingiras*, "huts," of his friends and shared with them milk from the native drinking gourds. In turn, he invited the tribal children to the stone bungalow to hear the bagpipe strains of the "Bluebells of Scotland" that came from the awesome Gramophone horn. The strange music was considerably different from the war cries they had heard issuing from the buffalo horns of their fathers.

He learned a number of other lessons as well. One day when he was six he found out that he wasn't much of a chemist. He had seen his mother make a pink antiseptic solution by adding a few grains of potassium permanganate to water. It looked so simple that the future scientist decided to dump a spoonful of the crystals into a cream jug of water. While he was trying to figure out why the solution had turned a dark reddish purple he heard the sound of footsteps behind him. In his haste to hide the jug he spilled the liquid on the sideboard cloth. It burned a hole right through it.

As his suspicious mother looked at the telltale jug and the scorched fabric, Louis vigorously insisted that he had nothing to do with it. It was simply Kikuyu magic. His father settled the matter by giving him his first spanking.

Seminars on the Verandah

It was in 1909 that Louis learned a lesson on the power and danger of the outdoors. After class one day he was playing in an acacia tree covered with the creeping passion fruit plant. As he was climbing, the remains of a dead leaf lodged in one of his eyes. He ran home and his mother tried to soothe the pain with a solution of boric acid. But in a few days the eye became infected. When it spread to the other eye, suddenly he lost all sight. The boy was terrified. Fortunately a doctor had recently retired to a farm nearby, and after Dr. Marsh had stopped the infection, the boy's eyesight gradually returned.

For a short time after this incident Louis stayed close to home. One day, while sitting on the verandah while his father prepared a sermon, he saw a familiar figure coming up the path. It was the witch doctor, wearing a cloak of gray baboon hide with war rattles dangling from his legs. He waved a bushbuck-tail fly whisk decorated with magic beads. As he smiled he showed the ivory fangs that had been put in to replace his teeth. Around his neck was an iron chain necklace holding two antelope horns. He carried a gnarled staff with the head of a rhinoceros carved in the wooden handle. To the boy he was just another citizen of the village.

To his father the tribal elder presented a serious problem. The man's practice of witchcraft had a powerful influence on the Kikuyus, and it made any attempt to convert them to Christianity a difficult task. But Harry Leakey knew that it was also important to maintain a cordial relationship with him. He greeted the old man. He had to respect the witch doctor's position in the community and at the same time work against him.

Years later Louis was to have a similar problem. He would run into frustrating labor trouble on his anthropological expeditions when the Kikuyu workers refused to touch ancient bones for fear of a malevolent tribal spirit. The witch doctor had long spread the word that anyone who disturbed the remains of the dead would be severely punished.

Another practice that disturbed the Leakeys was the killing of wild animals. Even as a child of six Louis was greatly disturbed by this. Though he hunted, he was concerned about natural history and the extinction of game. One day when Louis was sitting on the verandah with a friend, he saw a tribesman carrying a stool made from an elephant's foot. His face clouded and the native boy asked him, "Have you seen an evil spirit?"

Louis shook his head. "I don't like to see elephants killed," he answered.

The Kikuyu youth didn't understand. "It is a great day," he said, "when *tembo* is speared. There will be *nyama* for all."

"But," Louis protested, "my father told me that if you keep killing elephants there won't be many left."

Harry Leakey, standing behind them, smiled approvingly. He was glad to see that his son showed the same

11

affection for God's creatures that he was trying to teach at the Kabete Mission. He was pleased that the boy was equally at home with both black and white friends. Furthermore, he looked forward to the time when Louis would follow in his footsteps and spread the word of the Gospel. What he didn't see was the stubborn thrust of the young boy's chin and his growing independence. Louis was to have a strong mind of his own.

The Kikuyus both liked and respected the Leakey family. As a mark of their regard for the minister they had nicknamed him *"giteru,"* or "big beard." Kikuyus tend to have much less facial hair than Caucasians. Harry Leakey's full beard appeared rather odd to the Kikuyus. Years later they offered to give Louis what they called a mud shave. This meant coating the hair on his chest with mud clay and pulling the dried hair out, roots and all. Louis cordially refused.

The Kikuyu attitude toward the other British of the area was not always so friendly. Following the death of Queen Victoria, living conditions in Great Britain became very hard particularly for the working people. More and more of them left their homes to come to the British Colony of Kenya especially after the railroad between Mombasa and Nairobi had been opened.

These settlers followed the path of an earlier English explorer, Lord Delamere. As a farmer he believed that the land of the black man could easily become a white man's Garden of Eden. Without consulting or compensating the Kikuyu the settlers took over the lush highlands and carved them up into farms. Although the white settlers did bring some of the trappings of Western civilization to the area, and although their medicines doubled the local population by stopping disease and their advanced agricultural methods increased the food supply, they made the Kikuyu pay a great price for these improvements.

Louis Leakey would find himself involved in the consequences of this early exploitation. Years later, caught in the savage Mau Mau uprising of his Kikuyu brothers against his own countrymen, he would find it difficult to take sides. Fifty years later the districts would again be returned to the Kikuyu when Kenya became an independent African country. But *Uhuru,* "freedom," would be gained only after a long period of battle between these original antagonists.

In these first days of widespread colonization many Kikuyu, instead of farming the ancestral lands, found themselves working for a white stranger who might live in a cottage with an unlikely name such as "Pussywillow Farm." A displaced Kikuyu could be singled out by his green patched suit, striped cotton shirt, an old horse-racing cap and tennis shoes with holes. His wife, once the helpmate of a proud warrior, might wear the torn cotton dress discarded by her white mistress. It was a time of resentment and humiliation for some of the Kikuyu. And the six-year-old lad wasn't blind to it.

Growing up among the Kikuyu, he learned to respect their tribal culture. He also became intimately acquainted with their rituals and beliefs. He liked to sit and watch the tribal ceremonies as thousands of men linked arms to dance to the spirits who controlled their lives. On a moonlit night, surrounded by the clicking of bead necklaces and the chanting and the tapping of drums, he felt the fury or joy of their quick steps, the sadness or comfort of their slow ones. Looking down protectively over the tribesmen dressed in their lion and leopard skin cloaks was the Kikuyu god, Ngai, who sat benevolently on the top of a sacred mountain. It was not strange or alien to the young white Kikuyu. It was part of his life.

The time came too quickly when he would have to leave Africa for three years. The Leakeys were ready for another period of rest and travel. On Boxing Day, at the end of 1910, they took the train to Mombasa and boarded a steamer for England. After a long sea voyage during which Mary Leakey became very ill, they arrived at Louis's grandmother's house in Reading. Because of his mother's illness they were to stay much longer than planned.

Harry Leakey took over a job as schoolmaster at Gorse Cliff School in Boxcombe. He also enrolled his son in the preparatory school to give him some formal grounding in academic subjects. Louis mixed well enough with his English classmates, but he was homesick for his Kikuyu friends. The highpoints were the Saturday visits he made with his father to the Museum of Natural History in London. Although he passed the impressive statue of Charles Darwin in the lobby many times, he paid little attention to it. Still he was to become a strong disciple of Darwin, and the nineteenth-century naturalist was to have a major influence on his future life. At the age of seven, however, Louis was far more interested in the animal exhibits, particularly an elephant mother with her baby, which was displayed across the hall. Louis liked the museum for it reminded him of his home in Kenya.

May 1913, was a happy time for the Leakeys because they returned to Kabete. They brought with them a Miss Bull, a London graduate well-educated in the classics, to teach the children Latin and Greek. She was not ready for the kind of free and easy classes that were held on the verandah, which was hidden from the road by a high mukungugu hedge. She couldn't appreciate that what happened in the bush was as interesting to the children as what was taught in her formal class.

Because of this frustrating hedge Louis couldn't always see what was going on in the area. While conjugating Latin verbs he might miss the gyrations of a dancing baboon. But there was other wild life to distract his attention from language and mathematics. Rose bushes, verbena, and the thick bushes surrounding the house held a variety of animal activity. Louis became particularly interested in birds and began to study them closely and collect their eggs. He told her he wanted to be an ornithologist, a scientist who studies birds. Miss Bull didn't share his enthusiasm for nature study. By her standards the unruly children weren't accomplishing much in the way of traditional education.

One morning while the young Leakeys were hard at work declining Latin nouns, they heard a sharp, crackling sound. Miss Bull glanced up and returned to the lesson. But she had lost her students. They jumped to their feet and ran into the yard to see a long-awaited event. They arrived just in time to watch tiny fledglings emerge from their shells. Miss Bull ran after the children. Despite much grumbling on their part, she managed to herd them back to the porch to continue the lesson.

Another day the class was even more disrupted. Out of a corner of his eye Louis had been watching a chameleon climbing a nearby flower stem. He saw the reptile's tongue dart out to catch bluebottle flies. Suddenly a bright green snake emerged from the leaves and caught the chameleon. Louis couldn't sit still as the battle between the two animals turned into a life and death struggle. Finally in exasperation Miss Bull called a native boy to kill the snake. An argument followed. The children didn't want the snake killed. A compromise was reached. The snake was held while the chameleon scampered to safety. The animal was saved. Miss Bull impatiently dismissed her pupils.

The children were delighted when Miss Bull was replaced by a young teacher from Natal, the energetic and attractive Miss Broome. She quickly won favor by scrambling over the countryside in search of bird's nests and animal lairs, and shared in the imaginative life the young Leakeys had created around their favorite haunts. One day they took her to Bogojee, a stream near the mission site. They introduced her to the three lovely waterfalls they had incorporated in a fairy game. Each child had his own waterfall, Louis was lord of Doggish, Gladys was mistress of Cattish, and Julia, the oldest, was queen of Gibberish, the highest one shaded by ancient fig trees. The queen's palace was the largest tree, and Louis had to request permission to crawl into its huge hollow trunk to consult with the prime minister, Mr. Nobody. Miss Broome loved the place, and the children were only sorry that there were no more waterfalls for her to reign over. On another excursion, years later, Louis was to find a Stone Age relic in this same spot, the kingdom of Gibberish.

The verandah classroom became a joy for Louis. Miss Broome made the lessons so interesting that he even came to like Latin and algebra. But suddenly the children lost their teacher. She left to nurse the wounded in World War I. From then on they had to teach themselves, for during the war years Mary and Harry Leakey had little time to supervise their studies.

With the daily life of the village disrupted, Harry Leakey had his hands full. He did his best to allay the fears of the Kikuyu about the war. In the midst of flying rumors he assured them that the Germans had not taken over the railway line and that the zeppelins were not going to bomb East Africa. There were other problems as well. Many of the tribesmen had volunteered to defend the German-British boundary but others were forced against their will to serve as "carriers" in the war zone. Frightened inhabitants frequently asked Harry Leakey to intercede with the *Makanga,* or black tribal police.

Louis did his share in translating letters written by the "carriers" to their families in the village and in wrapping presents to be sent to the fighting zone. Because of the war he had more time to spend outdoors with his animals. The Leakey menagerie included, in addition to numerous dogs and cats, a duiker, which is a small antelope. It usually preferred to eat mulberry leaves and sweet potato vines, but it occasionally varied its diet by chewing the heads off chickens. After one such rampage Harry Leakey relegated the culprit to the "prison compound," where it joined a galago or "bush baby," a tree hyrax, a serval cat, and a Thomson gazelle in a fenced area.

At one point Louis decided he wanted a leopard cub as a pet. He had talked to native boys who crawled into the leopard caves when the mother leopards were absent and brought the cubs home. Louis's father vetoed the idea, because there was always the danger that the female leopard would come into the village searching for her offspring. Louis had to settle for more harmless pets.

His favorite was a Colobus monkey. He acquired it in a dramatic way. While he was having lunch one afternoon he heard excited voices on the path. He ran from the table and joined a group of tribesmen standing around something. He could hear a sound somewhere between a grunt and a roar coming from the middle of the crowd. When he

ploughed his way through the group he saw a man drag-
ging a Colobus monkey by its tail. The creature was in
pain and kept snatching at the arm of his tormentor.

Louis managed to take the animal away from the man
and took it back to the bungalow. His father made a large
cage out of old packing boxes. Louis, struck by the resemblance of the monkey to a human being, called it Christopher Columbus. With his white face and black head the
monkey looked like a dignified old gentleman with a skull
cap. For the next eight months the boy and the animal
were inseparable.

A Warrior Grows Up in the Bush

Louis was no stranger to the huge expanse of bush beyond the village. Tribesmen had taught him to be cautious and watchful in the bush. They had told him that his life depended on the ability to identify a paw print, to determine how near he had come to predatory animals. It was necessary to note that the motion of an elephant's ear could signal whether the beast was angry, and that if no breeze were blowing and yet leaves were stirring in a thicket a lioness might be hiding ready to pounce.

Besides the tutoring by the elders, there was an old tribal hunter and trapper who took Louis as a pupil. Joshua Muhia was possibly a member of the Ndorobo, a small nomadic tribe that hunted with bows and arrows and captured elephants in pits with harpoon and spear. He taught Louis to track and made him familiar with the habits and calls of all the animals of the area. Through him Louis learned a way of life that hadn't changed since prehistoric times.

It was on one of these green wild days that Muhia showed the young white Kikuyu how to trap with a rope and noose. When the Ndorobo warrior found a tree with the right kind of bark he broke off a large branch. He peeled off the outside bark, which was dry and brittle. Inside the bark it was soft, and he gave it to his young companion to chew until it was properly shredded. Then he showed him how to roll the pulp between his hands and thigh until it was elongated and had stiffened into a strong rope. Like a Stone Age man, Louis had made a hunting weapon without the help of a tool of civilized societies.

Another day Joshua showed him how to stalk a wild creature such as the duiker. He explained that they could not confront the animal directly, for it would dart away into the underbrush. A careful plan was necessary to trap the swift antelope where it usually slept.

Joshua built a low fence of branches around three sides of the duiker's resting ground. He left the fourth side open. They waited together until the unsuspecting animal returned and hid itself in the bush. The Ndorobo disguised himself with boughs and began cautiously to approach the wary duiker. He held his hands tightly at his sides. To the antelope these two appendages marked the weapons of a familiar enemy. At the slight movement the duiker raised its head. Reassured that the hunter was only a tree it lay down again.

Joshua slowly inched forward. At the last moment the startled animal saw the tree go into action. The duiker tried to escape to the far end of the fenced-in area where it was slowed down by running from one side to another. Joshua dropped his camouflage and threw himself on the duiker. On a later occasion, when Louis tried it, hurling his body on the terrified prey, he felt for the first time the passion of hunting. As he once said, he was both frightened and fascinated by the inexplicable wild instinct that overwhelmed him, an emotion he knew was as old as the human species. Years later, in remembering this time, he couldn't believe that he had actually enjoyed the sensation. But he realized that the difference between civilized and primitive people is the ability to recognize this desire and to control it.

Most of the time, however, the young hunter used his newly acquired skill to catch hares, porcupines, and moles. These predators were a tremendous nuisance to anyone raising poultry, and he took over the job of protecting his father's fowl yard. In addition to saving the family chickens, he also sold the skins of wild cats, mongoose, and genets in the *dukas* of Nairobi. Through the newspaper he found other markets as well. A zoo in India paid him for his African birds.

In those adolescent days of the hunt he set out to trap a strange adversary, the aardvark. This African anteater was a common enough animal, which could be found digging holes in search of white ants throughout the area. With its powerful forelegs and long claws it could dig as quickly as a person with a spade.

The harder Louis dug the more entrenched became the aardvark's hold in its subterranean chamber. Boy and beast went at it for several hours, each determined not to give into the other one. Louis's dander was up in not being able to gain any ground on the aardvark. Finally, at his wit's end and totally frustrated by his complete failure, Louis put some gunpowder and a fuse in a jam tin and set it off in the hole. Even though the gunpowder caused the aardvark to stop digging, it fought back for another quarter of an hour. To mark his victory Louis kept the skin and gave the meat to the natives. He sent the skull to the museum in Nairobi.

At this time Louis was as much Kikuyu as he was English. His best friend, Ishmael, was already an adult in the eyes of his parents. He now had his own living quarters. Louis wanted the same privilege. He told his father that he wanted to build his own hut, where he could be by himself and study his growing bird collection. By now Harry Leakey was well aware of his son's determination, and in order to keep him at least close to home, he consented if the hut would be built nearby. He gave the boy a plot of land that he had planted with wattle trees at the end of the garden.

When Louis was finished there was barely enough room to turn around in the one-room structure. Louis planted a garden of flowers, sweet potatoes, maize, and peas. But it was clearly inadequate for a domicile. So the next year he planned another building. With money earned from his trapping the white Kikuyu bought materials for a three-room house.

With the help of Kikuyu boys he cleared the grounds, cut down tree poles for the foundation, and slashed away at dry banana bark for the roof. *Matharara,* "banana leaves," were woven together with small, thin withies (branches) to form the walls. With everything completed except for a door and windows, Louis threw a house-warming party for the other workers. At last he had his own place, and he told his father that he would be living there from now on. Harry Leakey was far from enthusiastic, for the hut was damp and offered little protection from the weather. After much discussion, they agreed that Louis could use it for a daytime study but would return to the bungalow at night. Later he built a third hut.

Nevertheless, Louis spent most of his time there and at the hut of his friend Ishmael. They talked about their coming initiation into the tribe. Louis qualified for the honor because he had mastered the skills and had learned the tribal lore necessary to become a Kikuyu warrior. He was exceptionally competent at sword play with sticks, the throwing of clubs, and the intricate game of spearing a hoop at great distances.

In this ancient tribal game six highly competitive players on each side compete in what is really an exercise in hunting and war. To be on the winning side, which took the most prisoners, Louis had to hit a small target, both moving and stationary, with his spear. In addition, he had to be a fast runner, so if captured he could escape.

The day arrived when the young Englishman, his face etched with sacred white chalk, was inducted as a warrior into the Kikuyu tribe. Because of his keen eyesight, the chief gave him the name Wakaruigi, "Son of the Sparrow Hawk." The ceremony, celebrated by four days of feasting, dancing, and singing, marked the victory of the spirit of the adult over the child. As Wakaruigi passed under the arch of sugarcane and banana leaves, the tribal elder called down the blessing of Ngai. Louis did not accept the will of the Kikuyu god on the sacred mountain to worship ancestral spirits. Ingrained in him was the spiritual faith of his father and mother. The new warrior took an oath to contribute to the *Mzuri,* "good," of the tribe and never to reveal any tribal secrets. In fact, even in later years, Louis Leakey never revealed to anyone the secret rites of the Kikuyu.

Louis, now thirteen, appeared to want to devote his life to the study of birds. But at Christmas time a present came from a cousin in London that changed all that. It was a book that contributed to a chain of events that would cause the white Kikuyu to lower his eyes from the intense African sky to the ground where his prehistoric ancestors once walked.

Wakaruigi Enters the Stone Age

Late one afternoon in December of 1915, Louis sat in the study room of his hut, a pet monkey perched on his shoulder. He finally had time to open the gift book, Hall's *Days Before History*. Although familiar with the Greeks and Romans, he had never read about a time dozens of centuries before even the earliest civilizations. Louis eagerly turned the pages that told about prehistoric people who lived in the Stone Age many thousands of years ago. Neolithic people, much like the tribal people of Kenya, dwelt in huts of wattle and daub or mud and clay. In a way it was familiar, and in a way it was almost unbelievable. Certainly, he realized, it contradicted the Bible. Many theologians believed that the creation of man and woman as described in the Book of Genesis took place in about 4004 B.C.

But the author provided convincing proof. The stone tools that Neolithic people had left behind proved that people had lived on this planet much longer than 6,000 years. He was particularly fascinated with the idea that they hunted with arrowheads and ax-heads, and that many of these artifacts made of flint still remained. When he put the book aside to go to supper he was determined to find some of these ancient tools for himself.

After grace had been said and the family meal served, he brought up the subject of flint arrowheads. His father was surprised.

"But you don't even know what flint is," he advised his son.

"All I know," Louis replied, "is that it's blackish. If I found black stones of the right shape they might be arrowheads."

When Louis left the table to continue reading, Harry Leakey warned him that he had more important studying to do. Both his parents wanted him to enter Cambridge and prepare for the ministry. But it was already too late for that hope. The next day Louis was in the field searching for traces of Neolithic people who used Stone Age implements.

He walked briskly with Ishmael across the countryside, carefully scrutinizing the ground. After a few hours the Kikuyu became disgusted. "How can you look for something," he asked his friend impatiently, "when you don't even know what it is?"

"I'll know it when I see it," was Louis's only response. Finally when he was about to give up he found some bits of black stone beside the road. He examined them closely. "This is flint," he declared. "This is what I've been looking for. I read in a science book that flint is a dark kind of quartz and very hard."

Over the next few days he collected every piece of black stone he could find. When he brought them home, his father looked at them dubiously.

"No," Harry Leakey said. "I'm sure this isn't flint at all."

Louis had always had a deep respect for his father's

knowledge. "There must be someone in Nairobi," he said, "who can tell me definitely."

His father thought a moment. "What about Arthur Loveridge?" he asked. "You know him very well. He's been here a number of times. Since he's a curator at the museum he may be able to tell you something."

Louis was delighted with the idea. Loveridge, a good friend, had taught him a great deal about nature, how to blow the eggs of birds, how to skin and classify them according to their Latin names. But he hesitated about going to the small museum building in Nairobi. He hated to be wrong. Fortunately his curiosity was stronger than his pride, so that when Loveridge was next in Kabete, Louis showed him the stone tools.

As it turned out, Arthur Loveridge was quite pleased with his young friend's new interest. "I'm not an expert on prehistoric tools," he told Louis, "but I do know one thing. This stone is obsidian and was used by Stone Age people to make tools. Whether these are actually arrowheads I can't tell."

"And what is obsidian?" Louis asked, knowing nothing whatever about geology.

"It's a black glass formed from molten lava," Loveridge explained. "After it flows from the volcano it cools and hardens into stone. But come see for yourself at the museum. I have some arrowheads that were brought in by a member of the Society."

Some time later Louis hiked the eight miles to the Natural History Society. Loveridge took Louis over to a display case, and the young man studied them closely. "This is exactly the same as the stones I collected in Kabete," he commented.

Loveridge nodded. "I know. Some of your tools look very much like arrowheads."

When Louis returned to the mission he was much encouraged. He expected to find the ancient tools strewn across the countryside. It didn't occur to him that he would have to dig for them, that implements that had existed for so many thousands of years would more than likely be buried within the earth. Finally, when he had no success, he decided to know more about the whole subject. He went back to the museum, and Arthur Loveridge gave him books and articles about the Stone Age weapons of the European discoveries. He learned that, besides the Neolithic people who lived in huts, others inhabited caves. Several early people utilized flint found on the ground and by flaking the stone made sharp-pointed cleavers and hand axes.

After reading this, Louis decided to look in caves for stone tools. The first one that came to mind was the one near Gibberish Falls, where he had played his childhood games. Accompanied by his sisters he began the march to the point where the Bogojee and Mathare rivers met and formed the three magnificent waterfalls. As the three explorers climbed over the rocks Julia stumbled, and almost fell into a deep cavity in the side of a hill. Louis and Gladys came running to her aid and cleared some bushes away to rescue her. After she was safely out, Louis peered into the dark cave. He couldn't see to the bottom. He went off to find a goat herder who might know what was in it.

When Louis had explained what he wanted the old Kikuyu frowned. The witch doctor had told him that a huge, horrible snake lived at the bottom of the cavern with other wild beasts. Whenever a goat fell into the cave the Africans were afraid to go after it. But, he told the young man, there was another entrance at the bottom of the waterfall. If he dared, he might try that.

Louis and his sisters hurried down the path to find the entry by the edge of the stream. They already knew the spot. It had once been a lair for hyenas. But when they found the entrance choked with bushes they knew that the dangerous animals had left to find another site. All that Louis could see were the harmless tracks of mongooses and porcupines and other small animals. It would be perfectly safe to explore the cave.

So excited he couldn't sleep, Louis was up early the next morning to make a rope ladder with which to lower himself into the hole. At the insistence of his father, two Kikuyus went with him. That afternoon, armed with a a lamp and a spear to ward off any of the witch doctor's snakes, they left with Louis for Gibberish Cave.

When they arrived one of the natives, fearful of meeting a giant python, reluctantly descended to the dark cave floor. When he returned, greatly relieved to still be alive, he reported that the cavern was as large as a house and completely free of wild animals. Louis impatiently climbed down to have a look for himself. There was enough light from a crack in the rock wall to investigate the area, but he couldn't find any evidence of Stone Age man. He admitted, once back on the surface, that he had expected to find flint tools lying about on the ground.

Undaunted, he organized another expedition to another cave. Again in the company of several tribesmen, and carrying a sheath knife, torch, and matches, Louis approached a long narrow crevice that ran along the face of a lava cliff near the waterfall. Pushing a long stick as far as he could reach into the hole he couldn't touch bottom. He set fire to some dry grass at the end of the stick and peered into the tunnel, which seemed to make a sharp turn to the right.

Determined to see what was around that corner he

28

crawled into the hole, but it was so narrow that he couldn't even kneel down. He had to drag his body forward by gripping the rough floor with his outstretched hands. When he finally managed to round the corner he found himself at a dead end, faced by a wall of rock. Desperately, he realized that he couldn't reverse his way out. When he screamed for help a Kikuyu crawled in after him and gripped his ankles. Another helper outside followed him and, in turn, grabbed his legs. Slowly and painfully the human chain was extricated from the narrow crevice. But worse than the shock and the skinned arms and knees was Louis's disappointment. He still hadn't found a single piece of flint.

On a second expedition to Gibberish Cave, Louis did find, after a painstaking search, one small obsidian flake. Brought to the surface by the burrowing of a porcupine, the small volcanic rock was enough to fire his imagination. He was more convinced than ever that Stone Age man had indeed made this waterfall his home. Nevertheless he couldn't ignore the fact that the stone tools would not be easy to find. A true sign of the future anthropologist was that, even after so many failures, he was still determined to pursue the search.

The war was still going on, so the Leakeys were unable to make their usual trip to England. This gave Louis almost six years with little else to do but explore the countryside.

With his friend, Karugi, who had kept the charcoal brazier going the night he was born, he often hiked as much as fifty miles in a day. He slowly began to increase his collection of stone tools. Furthermore, he built up exceptional strength, a physical conditioning that would be of great value in the future. With the end of the war, however, came the end of this period of his life. When he ran across the countryside joyfully inviting the villagers to a Thanksgiving service to celebrate the German surrender he knew that he would shortly be back in England. In fact the Great War changed the trend of his life, for it firmly established his intent to study anthropology. If he had gone to England earlier he would have had the typical English youth's education that might well have turned him toward missionary work with bird study as a hobby.

On the day of departure in the summer of 1919, Waka-ruigi found it difficult to say good-bye to his best friend, Ishmael. The young warrior, already sixteen, was about to get married. Louis consoled himself that even if he were to stay things wouldn't be the same. The Kikuyu would remain, raise a family, and farm his tribal lands. Louis would go back to Britain and prepare to take a future degree in anthropology at Cambridge. Certainly few students there came from a more unusual background than the young Louis Leakey. And certainly few would ever find the world of British education more divorced from his own experience. If there was to be a continuity, Louis would have to create it himself.

Tight Fit of a Scholastic Hat

In January of 1920, Louis Leakey found himself walking in the winter sun across the campus of Weymouth College. A handsome young man, strongly built, with a deep African tan, his manner was easygoing and his personality inclined to friendship. Unfortunately none of this helped him. He had only been in the school building a short while when the prep bully jumped on him. The rugged outdoor boy easily "fought and kicked" off his attacker, but when the bully's friends saw that their champion might take a shellacking they joined the battle. When they were through with the newcomer they had locked him in a dismal coal hole in the boiler house. Luckily for Louis, a student prefect found him and decided to offer his official protection.

Louis was grateful to the prefect, but had a great deal of trouble taking orders from him. Although the prefect was six months older than Louis, the younger boy felt older in experience. He rebelled at the dozens of arbitrary rules imposed on him. For instance, he was forced to be in bed at a certain hour and to secure a pass to go shopping in town. Worst of all, he had to wear a much detested school uniform. As he wrote years later in his book, *White*

African, Louis Leakey commented: "I was being treated like a child of ten when I felt like a man of twenty and it made me very bitter. I was not understood as an individual nor treated as such." One feels that this observation is a considerable understatement.

Leakey did not make friends at Weymouth. On a Sunday afternoon the lonely schoolboy could be seen, attired in the regulation dark suit and straw hat, walking to Lodmoor Swamp. Through his field glasses he learned to pick out British birds by their plumage and their distinctive song. The relatively sparse bird populations only brought to mind, however, the rich bird life of the African bush and lake country. And bird watching was not a respected activity for young men at Weymouth. To others, it only made him seem more odd.

Louis suffered from another problem. Since the lakes of East Africa were full of crocodiles, he had never learned to swim. Thus he couldn't compete with those students who, raised by the sea, excelled in water sports. Also, accustomed to the strenuous exertions of the various Kikuyu games, he found cricket too tame. He often fidgeted around and became distracted while waiting to field a ball coming in his direction. Even though he was in fact a natural athlete, he was at a loss playing rugby. No one had bothered to explain the rules to him. He had played a far rougher sport at Kabete, had even organized a Junior Association Football Team in which he had kicked the ball with bare feet. But here at Weymouth his boots felt leaden, and he soon lost interest. He was like a bear who had wandered into a herd of antelope. He couldn't fit in.

After awhile, however, his classmates accepted that he was not a usual English youth. He held his own in the classroom, doing well in mathematics, Latin, and French, but had trouble with Greek. It didn't help his standing or morale when they put him immediately into an advanced class translating Xenophon. To catch up on the Greek grammar he received permission to stay in the classroom studying long after the other students were in bed. He was determined on getting a scholarship to Cambridge University. He needed the scholarship as he couldn't live on the small allowance that his father could provide.

In spite of his isolation at Weymouth, Louis did find private moments of pleasure. He was delighted to learn that the site of the school had once been the grounds of Neolithic people. He often took the train to Maiden Castle and wandered around the immense ditches and dikes of the fortified hill. He visited the British Museum of Natural History. He made contacts there among experts and showed his findings to them.

He was introduced to books whose authors he had never heard of, but with whom he found an instant rapport. One such writer was the Scottish explorer, James Hutton, born in Edinburgh in 1726. The geologist believed that the present is a key to the past, and that the rocks which form the crust of the earth are continually changing. While some rocks had been formed by sediment on the sea bottom, others had been produced by the action of live volcanoes. Subsequent erosion revealed that in a layer of sedimentary rock which once had been deep beneath the surface of water or earth were fossilized plants and animals spanning a tremendous period of time. Studying these fossils was like reading pages in the earth's history.

Louis also read the books of Jean-Baptiste Lamarck, a French botanist, zoologist, and physicist of the eighteenth century. Lamarck believed that the fossil records, going back in time, showed the progress of living creatures from a lower to a higher state of complexity. Lamarck also set out to prove that geography and climate caused this development. Thus living things were forced to adapt to new surroundings, change their living habits, gradually evolve new body structures, and ultimately bring about new species. Lamarck's basic premise was that characteristics acquired in this way could be passed on to offspring. A frequently cited example is the long neck of the giraffe. According to Lamarck's ideas the animals that evolved into giraffes found it necessary to stretch in order to reach food in trees. All this stretching resulted in longer necks— an acquired characteristic. The longer neck would then be inherited by offspring.

Although Lamarck was later shown to be wrong in his idea of the inheritance of acquired characteristics, he did contribute much to the development of biological science. He had the courage to propose that living things undergo transformation through time and were not created all at once and exactly as they now appear—an approach to the concept of evolution that was well before such ideas were fashionable among scientists.

Before the idea of evolution could be accepted there had to be an understanding of the great age of the earth. And in Lamarck's time there were few people who had any idea of just how old the earth was.

Some early investigation that led to an understanding of the age of the earth was done by William Smith, a surveyor, born in 1769, who was called the "father of English geology." While he made no attempt to explain creation other than by a supernatural act, he did see continuity through time in the evolving forms. He felt that the most primitive forms existed in the oldest and deepest rock strata. As the fossils were found closer to the surface in later deposits, they showed the consequences of progressive change. By studying these rock layers it was possible to place the various periods in chronological sequence and get some idea of their age. It was also possible, he suggested, that lying embedded in yet undiscovered rock strata were the bones of extinct animals unknown to humans.

It remained for the Frenchman, Baron Georges Cuvier, a contemporary of Lamarck and Smith, to piece together what little evidence they had of past animal life. He found that complete skeletons were seldom discovered intact, but this pioneer in fossil study did set about matching the hundreds of scattered bones he found in rock quarries around Paris. The French paleontologist made some of the first speculative sketches of what he thought the original living animals looked like. While he agreed with the generally held opinion that all living things were created according to a divine plan, he didn't think that it necessarily followed that all creatures should have the same structures of skull, jaw, and backbone. Rejecting an old theory that there was a ladder of life, with humans reigning supreme at the top, he suggested that as animals changed they branched out into a number of new orders. In turn, each animal order evolved skeletal and body structures that would ensure its survival.

Closer to Louis's own time, and to his own particular interests, was Charles Darwin, the great English naturalist who lived from 1809 to 1882. Louis was delighted to find that this son of a clergyman was also an enthusiastic bird watcher and a terrible student of Greek. He read with interest Darwin's account of his momentous five-year voyage on the *H.M.S. Beagle*. Ideas gained on this adventurous trip eventually led to the formation of the theory that humans evolved over millions of years from lower forms of life. It was during an exploration into the life of the Galapagos Islands off the coast of Ecuador that Darwin was struck by the incredible variety and wonder of the

myriad forms of life. Later this fascination would culmi-
nate in Darwin's theory that humans and apes shared a
common ancestor.

This reading intensified Louis's interest in geology,
paleontology, and anthropology. He became aware that
there was great controversy in all of these fields. Many
questions remained to be answered about the links
between humans and the other animals. But these questions only served to increase his curiosity.

Meanwhile, with the passing years at Weymouth, Louis
faced the more immediate questions of graduation. He
was more determined than ever to study at Cambridge,
the university of Byron, Milton, Charles Darwin, and
moreover his own family. It was at the beginning of 1922
that an English master at Weymouth suggested that Louis
apply to St. John's College at Cambridge. With this
encouragement, he went to see his headmaster in order to
make plans for his entrance and a possible scholarship.
But when he sat down all his hopes were dashed.

The headmaster bluntly explained the requirements for
a tripos, the course of study for any honors degree. Mr.
Conway didn't waste any time disillusioning the young
man about a possible academic future.

"Your Greek is much too weak," he said frankly, "to
face the classical tripos. Your only other language is
French, and it takes two foreign languages for the modern
languages tripos. I don't see that there's any chance at all
in mathematics, science, or history. You could take an
ordinary tripos but that would be a waste of time."

Louis nodded in agreement. There was nothing he
could do, and it didn't help when he told the headmaster
that he would only have sixty pounds a year to pay
expenses at the university. Mr. Conway ended the inter-

view by suggesting that Louis forget about Cambridge and enter a bank. Louis left the office completely discouraged.

But the same stubbornness that Harry Leakey had early detected in his son was stronger than ever. A bizarre solution occurred to him. He did know another language besides French. He spoke absolutely fluent Kikuyu. Realizing that there could not possibly be anyone at Cambridge who could examine him in that African language, he submitted in accordance with university regulations a "certificate of competent knowledge."

It worked. The ancient university was unable to admit that there was a language spoken by over half a million people that they couldn't admit as a legitimate subject. They were willing to accept proof of Louis's fluency from a Kikuyu chief, who wrote that indeed the young man was a master of that exotic tongue. Finally in October he qualified for the modern language tripos, and the way was clear for Louis to take up residence at St. John's College. In fact, contrary to Mr. Conway's expectations, he did so well on his entrance examinations in Latin, French, and mathematics that he was awarded a sizarship of forty pounds.

The first year flew by. Louis was free again. He had his own room, cooked his own meals, and could come and go as he pleased. Unfortunately the term was marred by his attempt to cram into a one-year course two years of advanced French. He failed the subject and lost his scholarship for the coming year. Faced with a serious financial crisis he tried to earn money by tutoring, but there were no positions available. So that summer he took a job with a doctor's family in North Wales as the house cook. In his spare time he walked all over the countryside, enjoying the Welsh landscape.

When he got back in the fall of 1923 an accident occurred that ironically forced him further into his future profession. Louis had always wanted to play rugby and to win the coveted college colors. The chance came and he joined the team. But one day as he was playing what he later referred to as "the game of my life," a player accidently kicked him in the head. As a result of the injury, terrible recurrent headaches forced him to take a leave of absence from the university. His doctor ordered him not only to take a complete rest from books, but to find a spot where he would be in the open air most of the time. This was frustrating advice for a student who barely had enough money to live at Cambridge, not to mention taking an enforced vacation for a year.

As it turned out the incident was for the best. While at the university Louis had kept in touch with an old family friend now living in London. This collector of Stone Age artifacts informed him of a paleontological expedition getting underway to hunt for fossil reptiles in Tanganyika (now Tanzania). Mr. Hobley told him that the British Museum was looking for someone who knew East Africa from firsthand experience. He was certain that Louis could get a position with the group.

Louis could hardly contain his excitement when he received an invitation from the museum on January 29, 1924, to join the expedition. He would have a rare opportunity to search for dinosaur bones on Tendaguru Hill, a fossil site earlier explored by German scientists. He would also receive valuable practical experience working under a famous paleontologist, W. E. Cutler. Although Cutler was known to have one of the finest fossil collections in the world, he had never set foot on African soil. He welcomed the aid of a young British youth born in Africa who could supervise details of the expedition.

Cutler and Leakey sailed for Mombasa on February 28, 1924. While the older man went on to Dar es Salaam in Tanganyika to set up the expedition, Louis stopped in Kabete for a few days to visit his parents. Since they had not seen him in four years, his parents were amazed at how he had changed and matured. He was no longer Wakaruigi, the future missionary. He had become a promising scientist, but he assured them that he would always follow the teaching of the Lord.

The Tanganyika Expedition

In mid-March, when Louis met Cutler in Dar es Salaam, a Tanganyikan seaport, he learned that most of the supplies and equipment ordered in London had been held up by a dock strike. Cutler decided to remain in the capital to wait for the shipment. He asked Louis to go on ahead. He provided him with maps, plans, and photographs of the previous German expedition to Tendaguru Hill.

On the first lap of the trip Louis boarded a Dutch cargo boat to the village of Lindi about 250 miles down the coast to the south. Since there was no hotel in the small port of call, Louis sent a note with a letter of introduction to the port commissioner asking for a night's lodging. The word of mouth reply sounded promising so he briskly set out to follow a muddy track along the shore. Suddenly he found himself at the bottom of a ditch, covered with filth and torn by thorn bushes. Looking very disreputable he continued to the house, marched up the steps calling out "Hodi," which in East Africa is the same as knocking on the door, and was received by a very surprised Major Cadiz. He hadn't been expecting the young man for he had never received his message. He helped Louis to find quarters elsewhere.

After this inauspicious beginning things began to go better. Louis found temporary lodgings in an empty house with a camp bed and mosquito netting. From this base he visited the Indian shops to buy supplies—lanterns, cooking utensils, and medical stores. Since he was going into territory completely new to him, he spent a few weeks finding a competent guide for the long cross-country march. Once he had found him, the man, Jumbe Ismaeli, helped Louis to recruit fifteen porters to carry the equipment for the safari. Finally a cook and a gun-bearer were found to accompany the party from Lindi to Tendaguru Hill. Thus it wasn't until mid-April that the group began the overland trip through coconut plains and bush country to their eventual encampment.

The march proceeded well enough for several days until they reached a strip of land where it had been raining heavily. Even with hobnailed boots Louis was barely able to save himself from continually sliding down the slippery hillsides. It was even worse for the porters, who carried seventy-pound loads in mud up to their knees. It was a fatiguing, infuriating trip, and when the party finally called a halt for the night they were all covered with black mud. It was only the beginning of learning to live with discomfort, insects, bad weather, and difficulty with the local crew.

Fortunately the day before, Jumbe had sent a runner ahead to notify the local inhabitants that Mzungu, a white man, would be passing through their village. When the party arrived at Ntanga a tribal elder appeared to guide the safari to a grass rest hut where natives provided rice, eggs, bananas, and sugarcane. In return, Louis gave them gifts of calico cloth and beads, as well as medicine from his first aid supplies.

After three more days of trekking through the wild

African countryside the party moved through dense forest and then into open parkland. The going was easier until they reached heavy thickets of bamboo thirty feet high, and then they began the painfully slow process of hacking their way up the mountain. At the top of a cliff Louis could finally see his destination three miles away. The conical hill of Tendaguru looked exactly as shown in the photographs he had with him taken ten years before by the German explorers. When they arrived, Louis's party even found some trash of the previous group—a rusty sardine can and a broken beer bottle.

Jumbe spotted smoke from a fire several miles away and advised his employer to fire his rifle to announce the coming of a white man. Tribesmen answered the signal by bringing eggs and bananas for Mzungu and his hungry men. At sunset the headman beat out a drum call to the people of the district to bring knives and axes to help build a permanent camp.

That evening, sitting in the grass hut built for him in a village near Tapahira, Louis had mixed feelings of excitement and loneliness. Miles from any white man, he was camped in the middle of the African bush, the wild haunt of lions, leopards, and other dangerous game. Although he had successfully accomplished the first part of his assignment, he wished for a moment that he was back in the stone bungalow in Kabete hearing the familiar strains of the hymn, "Christ the Lord is Risen Today." It was Easter, 1924.

The next day Louis was up early to greet thirty natives who had come in response to the drum call. They cleared brush and dug postholes for the three-room hut Louis and Cutler would occupy for the next six months. When the comfortable thatched-roof bungalow made of bark, bamboo, and grass was finished, Louis set out with a few porters to meet Cutler in Lindi.

Though the return journey to Tendaguru went well and Cutler was a good walker, there were incidents along the way. Juma, the native headman, was proud of his service in the German army, and Louis let him carry a small gauge shotgun with a single barrel. However, Juma was not a gun expert. He thought it was a rifle. Late one afternoon as they were making their way through brush country a leopard sprang up. Juma jammed the gun into the beast's shoulder and fired point-blank. It was only loaded with dust shot, and although startled, the leopard didn't fall. Juma was amazed when the animal loped carelessly away unharmed. He couldn't believe that he hadn't killed it at that range. He warned them to go ahead with great caution because the leopard was charmed and, according to a tribal belief, was really a witch doctor who through black magic had taken the form of an animal.

There was no black magic involved when Cutler received his first introduction to the dangers of the African bush. When the safari rested for a few minutes under the shade of a mango tree he went off, against Louis's firm warning, to gather some unusual seed pods from a climbing bean plant. He tied them in a handkerchief, and later when he wiped his face the tiny seed hairs that had clung to the cloth were rubbed into his skin. He screamed with pain. The plant was poisonous. Louis applied some lotion, and after that Cutler was more cautious.

In mid-June, Cutler picked out the three main sites for excavating the fossils of dinosaurs that had roamed the area during the Jurassic period over 200 million years ago. A hundred local dwellers recruited by Louis acted as a digging crew. Although they were supplied with wheelbar-

rows for hauling the dirt away, they found a more conve-
nient way to carry it. Unable to adapt to the pushcarts,
they used the barrows as if they were the more familiar
baskets, and carried them on their heads.

Cutler and Leakey took over the job of removing the
fragile bones of an eighty-foot long dinosaur that they
found embedded beneath the ground. In the process Louis
learned a great deal about the techniques of excavation.
On his hands and knees he learned to dig with a trowel in
hard rock; to loosen the matrix—the material in which the
fossils were held—with an awl so as not to injure the
bones; and to sweep the loose earth away with a soft
camel's hairbrush. Cutler also taught him how to preserve
the fossilized bones by coating them with shellac and then
setting them in plaster. Before these modern methods
were used many precious fossils were lost. Great care had
to be taken because some of the fossils would crumble at
the slightest touch and could be ruined while being crated
and shipped to museums.

One afternoon the incredible aspect of what he was
doing struck Louis with particular force. As he sat resting
under a tree he could see printed on the sandstone wall a
few feet away the perfect shape of a palm leaf that had
existed millions of years before. It was almost unbelievable that the leaf had fallen, drifted on the wind, and settled
on the waters of a stream. Sinking slowly to the bottom, it
had become embedded in the silt to be covered by layers
of sediment. After the stream had dried up, the sediments
hardened into rock. Many millions of years were to pass
before the wind and rain began their process of erosion.
Layer after layer of rock was worn away until on this
peaceful day millions of years later the leaf was revealed,
its outline clearly preserved in the rock, to a young man

who would himself live but a fraction of a second of the earth's long history.

The dinosaur fossils that Louis observed demonstrated that large size and strength were no insurance for survival. These huge reptiles, the largest land animals that ever walked on the surface of this planet, had been outlasted by smaller and punier life forms. No one knows the full story of why dinosaurs became extinct. Dinosaurs of one kind or another were dominant life forms for about 200 million years, but the last of them were gone about 70 million years ago. Changing world conditions certainly contributed to the demise of the big reptiles. Smaller, warm-blooded animals could survive in the conditions that finished off the dinosaurs. And some of these warm-blooded animals evolved into forms that eventually led to the human species.

Louis almost lost his life a number of times by neglecting the real dangers of the beasts around him. Once, while he was trying to bag a covey of pigeons for dinner, he crawled into some thick bushes. Suddenly a thundering, rumbling sound told him that he was in the midst of a herd of elephants with their young calves. If they smelled him they would stampede to save their babies. Armed with only a small shotgun he waited, terrified for them to pick up his scent. Luckily the wind was blowing the other way, and he managed to creep quietly away before they could charge. Another day, while walking through the bush, he saw a tree snake poised on a branch, its head back ready to strike. In a flash he realized it was a maamba, the most deadly snake in Africa, its poison powerful enough to kill a man in seconds. As Louis leaped back in terror the snake struck, its flicking tongue missing his neck by a fraction of an inch. Barely taking aim he raised his gun and fired, blowing the snake to bits. A third close call took place in his tent. He was laid up with malaria when he became aware that a strange animal had entered the darkened enclosure. As he was too weak to call for help, he watched, frozen with fear, as a leopard came toward him. At the last moment it sprang, tore a pet baboon from his side and crashed away into the night.

Though dangerous, the expedition proved successful. At its conclusion Cutler told him that he had become an experienced fossil hunter. The renowned scientist was amazed at how quickly his colleague had learned all aspects of the job, and even commented that Louis was ready to lead his own expedition. He encouraged the young man to make paleontology his profession. But Louis was going through a period of great doubt. He was torn in his choice of a career. He knew that his parents expected him to become a missionary and return to Kabete to minister to the Kikuyu. At the same time, his interest in prehistory had become consuming. He admitted to Cutler that he didn't know what he would finally do.

The one thing that was clear was his immediate return to Cambridge. It was late October and he made plans to go back after an absence of almost a year. Cutler escorted him to Lindi, where Louis had booked passage on a coastal steamer to Dar es Salaam. From there he would take another ship sailing on November 16 to Mombasa, and have enough time for the voyage to England. But when they arrived in Lindi they learned that the *Dumra,* scheduled to sail on November 3, had been struck with boiler trouble and wouldn't leave for a week. It meant missing the other connecting vessels.

Completely floored, Leakey realized that he had only twelve days to reach Dar es Salaam. Furthermore, he saw there was nothing for him to do but walk the 269 miles cross-country to meet his sailing date for Mombasa. That plan involved a further delay, because Louis would have to hire at least fourteen porters and a headman for the safari. Thus on November 4 Louis said what turned out to be a last good-bye to his mentor and friend, for Cutler was to contract typhoid and malaria before returning to Tendaguru, and Louis never saw him again.

The trip to Mombasa was anything but a pleasant one. An Arab dhow that the men took to cross an arm of the sea got bogged down in tidal mud. Hippos and crocodiles continually attacked their canoes on another part of the trip. It was the dry season, and the party was wracked by a shortage of water and food. The danger of malaria was always present, and at one point they were overtaken by a violent rainstorm and left soaked to the skin and shivering with cold.

At last on November 16, after the most arduous journey of his life, Louis checked into the Burgher Hotel in Dar es Salaam. "Filthy and unshaven," he sank into a hot bath. It was more than having survived the trip. He was tanned and hardened by the outdoors, healthier and in a better state of mind than he had ever been. The headaches were gone. He had helped excavate valuable fossil remains and in addition had saved over seventy pounds for the coming year at Cambridge. He had even had the foresight to bring with him a collection of ebony walking sticks which he would later exchange with a London tailor for some proper clothes. Finally, the second year at the university looked hopeful.

After his return to Cambridge in the winter term of 1925, he was asked by the British Museum to give an illustrated lecture of his expedition to Tendaguru.

Although the possibility of earning some money interested him, he had second thoughts when he discovered that there would be at least a thousand people in the audience. The enormity of what he was about to do struck him when he passed the hall one morning and saw a series of posters, eight feet high, announcing in large letters the public address of Mr. L. S. B. Leakey of St. John's College, Cambridge. Suddenly the difficulties of the long march from Lindi dwindled in comparison to the prospect of giving his first speech. He didn't know enough about the subject. Famous scientists would be there. He imagined that his classmates would freely boo him if the evening was a failure.

The moment came when Leakey, terrified, found himself seated on the stage of the great hall surrounded by academic dignitaries. He had borrowed a tuxedo and white waistcoat and it didn't fit. He felt he looked ridiculous. As he watched the auditorium fill up his anxiety increased. The people chatted easily as they took their seats. They expected him to deliver an erudite, professionally prepared lecture. Minutes before he was introduced he was ready to bolt from the stage. But when the lights dimmed and the first slide came on the screen his terror suddenly vanished. He was back in the world he knew best, and with relief he realized that he really did know a great deal about the Tendaguru expedition. Discarding his notes, he began to speak confidently and after a few minutes knew the lecture was a success. Then something diverted his attention, he turned back to the audience, and was appalled to discover that he couldn't remember what came next. The lecture completely fell apart. Only the showing of a section of "The Lost World," a film about dinosaurs, saved him. He had meant to show it at the end but in his panic he jammed it in immediately. Many of the spectators wondered why the evening was so short.

In spite of his initial failure, the museum asked him to continue the lectures. It meant earning money, but more importantly he had a firm connection with the museum collections and staff. He began to spend more time there, and the possibility of his becoming a missionary disappeared.

His commitment to science was strengthened by his Sunday afternoon visits to the home of Dr. A. C. Haddon, the reader in anthropology at the University of Cambridge. During the vigorous give and take of these informal student discussions, he learned more than in the classroom. The most controversial topic of these stimulating meetings was Darwin's theory that all warm-blooded animals had evolved from one common ancestor millions of years ago. There was no hard fossil evidence to prove it. Many of the disputants seriously doubted that such remains would ever be found. It appeared that Darwin's concept would always be just that, an imaginative but unproved speculation. Years later Louis Leakey would be involved in a similar scientific controversy trying to convince a skeptical scientific community of the significance of his fossil finds.

Louis's association with Dr. Haddon was valuable in another way. The professor had an exceptional library, and his student often returned to his small room high under the gables of the Third Court of St. John's College with a pile of books under his arm. One such volume had a tremendous impact on the young scientist. It was *Man's Place in Nature,* written in 1863 by Thomas Henry Huxley, the man whose brilliant defense of Darwin greatly contributed to the widespread acceptance of the theory of evolution. In this book Huxley made it clear that not only did he accept Darwin's ideas on the evolution of mammals, but he also believed that this evolution applied to man as well.

In his book, *On the Origin of Species,* Darwin had limited his comments on the evolution of man to one sentence at the very end of the book, "Much light will be thrown on the origin of man and his history." In a later book, *The Descent of Man,* Darwin offered a full discussion of his ideas on human evolution.

Not surprisingly, this proposition brought the wrath of the religious communities and many scientists down on his head. It threatened the whole idea that man was a higher form of life, created by God, and having no natural kinship with the other animals. One bishop, thinking it the greatest possible insult, asked Huxley if he had descended from a monkey on his grandfather's side. The great interpreter of Darwin brushed the comment aside. The only question, he replied, was not whether there was an early ancestor of *Homo sapiens,* but whether such an ancestor had existed in the Pliocene or Miocene eras. However, in the middle of the nineteenth century very few fossils had been unearthed, and it would be left to future paleontologists to produce the evidence. Huxley had no doubt that it would be found.

The White African Confronts Man's Past

While Louis Leakey was at the university, interest in scientific exploration was being renewed after World War I had temporarily halted all field research. It was an exciting time as scholars turned with fresh enthusiasm to reconciling old theories about the origins of the human species with new data and ideas. An increasing number of traditional concepts had to be discarded as new information in the form of prehistoric bones and stone implements came to light. Sir Arthur Keith brought a significantly fresh approach to the study of man's past. He, and many others, were compelled to continually revise their conclusions as new fossil evidence was uncovered.

An expert in the reconstruction of prehistoric humans from fossil fragments, Keith had stood alone for years in believing that *Homo sapiens* had existed since early in the Pleistocene period. In 1915 he had taken the figures of W. E. Sollas on the recent ages of geology and produced a timetable of mankind. Working with geological information he placed the Pleistocene at 400,000 years ago and the Pliocene at one million years. Ten years later he changed his estimate and moved the Pleistocene back to one million and the Pliocene to approximately 11 million years.

This was how long man, as a distinct species, was believed by several scientists to have been on the earth.

In his book written in 1915, *The Antiquity of Man*, Keith proposed another idea that stirred the scientific community. He said that man's evolution over the ages had been made in a series of successive stages. He was convinced that Neanderthal man, whose remains had been found in Europe, was one of these stages. Although a primitive form of man, Neanderthal had a brain sometimes larger than that of modern man.

Many of the ideas put forth by Keith had been severely questioned. However, even though Keith was not too successful in proposing sound theories he did much to promote the science of human paleontology in the 1910s and 1920s. Keith had a profound influence on the young Louis Leakey. Leakey did not accept all of Keith's ideas, but Keith figured prominently in Leakey's decision to become a paleontologist.

When Arthur Keith became conservator of the Royal College of Surgeons in London, he filled the rooms with showcases of fossil relics. He welcomed students who might construct from these scattered remains the unifying theory he had been searching for most of his life. Under his guidance Louis Leakey made the final commitment to becoming an anthropologist and paleontologist.

On a furlough from Kabete in 1925 Harry Leakey visited his son at Cambridge. He was not pleased with Louis and they had it out. It was immediately evident to the father that his son's readings in science had completely replaced his allegiance to the church. The elder Leakey was very disappointed since he had always expected Louis to take orders and return to Kabete to continue missionary work. Even during his son's trip to Tendaguru he had considered this interest in anthropology merely a hobby.

But if he had any hopes of changing Louis's mind they were quickly dispelled. He was startled to hear the young man even question the dogma of the Church of England. Darwin, whom the father had regarded as a harmless naturalist, had become a dangerous influence. Harry Leakey adamantly insisted that man was created on the Seventh Day, and any attempt to disprove that was blasphemy. When Louis introduced fossil evidence his father shook his head in disgust. It was simply a theory, and like all scientific theories that conflicted with a fundamental reading of the Scriptures, it would be proved wrong.

Since there could not possibly be any agreement, Louis wisely let the matter rest. He was very fond of his father and respected his judgment in other areas. But he knew that the ordained minister was bound up in his biblical truths. There was no way at this point to change the older man's views. When Harry Leakey left, his son had a mixed feeling of exhilaration and sadness. He had broken his own link with the past. He was irreversibly set on a course.

He informed Dr. Haddon that he planned to take part two of the anthropology tripos the following year. Since he had earned a scholarship for the fall term he was free to devote the summer to visiting museums with prehistoric collections. On a motorcycle trip from Wales to Norfolk he examined countless exhibits and took copious notes. He searched for relics in the rich sites of East Anglia which dated back to the Pleistocene epoch. When he returned to Cambridge he settled down to study to be a scientist. During that year he was also introduced to the incredible tales of exploration that had come out of expeditions in Europe, Asia, and Africa in the previous century. His major interest was studying the history of anthropology.

Louis found out that the first human fossils to come to the attention of scientists were uncovered in Europe. The earliest of these were found by accident and attracted little attention among the scientific community. As early as the seventeenth century there were some pioneer prehistorians who proposed that chipped stones found with bones of extinct animals had been made by "primitive" men. In 1771 a German, Johann Esper, found human bones together with the remains of a type of cave bear that no longer existed.

The work of pioneers such as Esper was generally ignored for a number of reasons. There was little if any understanding of the age of the earth, and most people could not or would not accept anything that contradicted the biblical account of creation.

The earliest finds came about through the digging of ditches, and excavating for new buildings and other construction. Undoubtedly many human fossils were tossed into the dirt heaps. Among the first human fossil bones to attract the attention of scientists was a skull found in Gibraltar in 1848. It was not positively identified until 1900 when it was shown to be the skull of a Neanderthal man.

The term *Neanderthal* man comes from a valley in Germany. *Thal* means "valley" in German and the Neander is a river in Germany. Neanderthal means Neander valley and it was in this valley, near Düsseldorf, that a skull cap and some limb bones were dug out of a cave in some limestone cliffs in 1856. It was fortunate that the workman, surprised though he was, had the presence of mind to bring the bones to the attention of a local science teacher. The fossils then made the rounds of a number of scientists, including the well-known anatomist Rudolph Virchow, who declared that the bones were not primitive at all, but had belonged to a deformed person. Other scientists who examined the bones did not agree with Virchow and the matter lay unresolved for some thirty years. Neanderthal man was short compared to modern man. The average Neanderthal adult was a little over five feet tall. He had heavy brow ridges, no chin point, and rather robust limb bones.

More Neanderthal remains were found in diggings in a cave near the Belgian city of Spy in 1886. This time the human bones were found with the bones of several extinct mammals along with several chipped stone tools. The diggings had been carried out carefully so that the associations between the human bones, stone tools, and animal remains were unquestionable. The evidence uncovered at Spy could not be easily refuted. It was now certain that man of a type unlike modern man once trod the surface of this planet.

The news of the findings at Spy started a new wave of interest in looking for human fossils. Unfortunately much of this work was done by amateurs who frequently made shambles of what might have been a promising digging site.

Neanderthal man soon came to represent what most people thought of as "cave men." A popular picture of a club wielding, shuffling, grunting creature who was more beast than man emerged. The brain of Neanderthal man was as large or larger than human brains are today. This fact, together with later discoveries which shed light on Neanderthal's way of life, tended to contradict the image of this form as a rather brutish, subhuman who, in fact, lived as recently as 40,000 years ago.

Discoveries made in 1908 at Le Moustier in southern

France indicated that Neanderthal may have had some rather sophisticated thoughts. The bones of a Neanderthal teenager were found here, but it was the circumstances in which they were found rather than the bones themselves that commanded the interest of the diggers. The boy had obviously been buried in a very careful manner. He had been carefully placed on his side with his head cushioned on a "pillow" of flaked flints. His arms were folded as if he were asleep. A number of stone tools and animal bones had been buried with him. Other Neanderthal "cemeteries" have been found. At one site at La Ferrassie, also in southern France, what appeared to be an entire family of two adults and four children were found buried in a cave floor. They had all been buried in an east-west orientation. The inclusion of tools in graves would seem to indicate that Neanderthal had enough intelligence to develop a concept of life after death. There is also some evidence, not fully accepted by all anthropologists, that Neanderthal may have fashioned objects for their artistic, rather than practical value.

A lower jaw found in Germany in 1907 gathered a great deal of interest and created even more confusion. This so-called Heidelberg jaw was not like the jaws of Neanderthal that had by this time been found in relative abundance. Just what kind of creature is represented by the Heidelberg jaw has still not been determined. The debate and confusion over the Heidelberg jaw was only a taste of what was to come as more and more paleontologists and anthropologists dug up more ancient human bones and tools. Every new find was and still is the trigger of heated controversy as the finder defends his ideas on the significance of his find. All of this is part of the scientific process. Every new fossil find is part of a puzzle, and it is inevitable that controversy will ensue as scientists try to determine where the new piece fits into the slowly emerging and changing picture of the history of humans.

Neanderthal was not the only type of fossil man found in Europe. In 1868, during the building of a railroad, some bones were uncovered near at Les Eyzies, Dordogne, France. The particular rock formation in which the bones were found is called the Cro-Magnon rock shelter. Thus this kind of man came to be called Cro-Magnon.

Cro-Magnon people were very much like modern people. If any Cro-Magnons were alive today their appearance would attract no attention. They were taller than Neanderthal people, had chin points and lacked the heavy Neanderthal brow ridges. Many anthropologists think that Cro-Magnon people may have originated in the Middle East and moved into Europe eventually displacing the Neanderthals.

The rich fossil finds in Europe during the nineteenth and early twentieth centuries led many anthropologists to believe that man originated in that continent. For a while Louis Leakey was among those who thought that Europe was the place where the human species had begun. But class discussions at Cambridge brought to his attention startling discoveries in Asia. They were initiated by a young Dutchman, Eugène Dubois, who had studied Neanderthal fossil remains in Europe. While a medical student at the University of Amsterdam he had been intrigued by Darwin's theory that early humans might still be found in areas of the world where the great apes still lived. Since the orangutans made their home in Asia, Dubois believed that primitive humans might once have inhabited this continent.

After Dubois became a lecturer in anatomy at the University of Amsterdam at the end of the nineteenth century, he decided to try to prove this theory. Since he didn't have enough money to finance such an expedition, the young professor took a position as an army doctor in the jungles of the Dutch East Indies (now Indonesia). In spite of his exhausting medical duties he managed to make a memorable trip to the small village of Trinil on the island of Java. With incredible patience he scoured the entire area. His efforts were rewarded in November of 1891 when he found a human tooth, skull cap, and some jaw fragments. A year later, at another location not far from the first, he uncovered a human femur bone and in 1891 a second tooth. Studying the fragments he concluded that the fossils had belonged to the same creature.

Most important, Dubois felt that the thigh bone belonged to an animal which stood erect and was able to swing his arms freely. But whereas the femur seemed human, the skull was monkeylike. There was almost no forehead and the jaw looked like the muzzle of an ape. At the time of his discovery he thought it might well be that this combination of man and ape could be the "missing link" he had hoped to find. He named the heavily built creature that had stood about five foot eight inches tall *Pithecanthropus erectus* (erect walking man), from the Greek words *pithecus* for "ape" and *anthropus* for "man." It was commonly referred to as Java man. Its official name is *Homo erectus*. Other *Homo erectus* fossils were found in China.

Louis marveled at this amazing discovery, which might have solved the mystery of man's origin. But the leading scientists were divided on their identification of the fossil teeth of the Java man. Some said they were human; others insisted that they were too apelike. Still others thought the bones belonged to an orangutan or a large gibbon. For quite some time Dubois remained unshaken by the controversy and continued to affirm that the animal was a hominid, or near man, which had lived 500,000 years ago. He became so annoyed with his critics that he locked his specimen up and refused to let anyone look at it.

The discussion over whether *Pithecanthropus* was human or ape went on for many years. It wasn't until 1915 that Leakey's highly respected teacher, Sir Arthur Keith, accepted it as representing an early stage of human evolution. When he concluded that all human races had descended from some common stock, in Asia, other authorities agreed with him. But all authorities agree that the human ascent from apelike animals to *Homo sapiens* was not clearly defined and further research was needed.

Although by 1924 most scientists had accepted Java man as the common ancestor of the modern human, Louis Leakey was becoming more convinced that human origins lay elsewhere. There had been impressive evidence in Africa. As early as 1867 tools of an early Stone Age type were found in Egypt and then at the other end of the continent near Capetown, South Africa. But in the following forty years most scholars had ignored these areas. Subsequent expeditions had turned up only skeletons of long-extinct baboons and apes. Besides, the overwhelming opinion was that man had come from either Europe or Asia. Anyone who seriously believed that Africa was the cradle of human life was considered either misinformed or a fool.

Still in 1910, two Germans, Max Schlosser and Richard Markgraf, did draw some attention to this neglected continent. Digging in the Fayoum Depression some sixty miles southwest of Cairo, Markgraf uncovered the lower jaw of an apelike creature. Schlosser proposed the name *Propliopithecus* in the mistaken belief that it was the ancestor of a creature called *Pliopithecus,* a form believed to be ancestral to the gibbon.

As so often happened, the next African finds went almost unnoticed. In 1913 the famous German geologist, Professor Hans Reck, conducted the first excavations in what was known then as the Oldoway Gorge in Tanganyika (now Tanzania). He dug up the remains of a human skeleton lying with its knees drawn up under its chin. The specimen was quickly rejected as not being old, as being a recent ancestor of the Masai tribe that lived in the area. Just before the outbreak of World War I a human skull fossil was also discovered in Boskop in the Transvaal Province of South Africa. It was also judged insignificant, simply a strange variant of Neanderthal man or one of the early *Homo sapiens* that had already been found in Europe.

The third find was taken more seriously, but there were still strong doubts. Part of a hip bone, two ends of a femur, and a skull were found in a lead mine at Broken Hill, Northern Rhodesia (now Zambia). The ancient cave was also full of what appeared to be Stone Age implements. When the cave deposits were dug up and sent to the British Museum in 1921 the experts poured over them. It was a slow process. Finally the verdict came in. Anatomists decided that this Rhodesian man was the first human of an extinct species ever found in Africa.

These unimpressive African relics hardly prepared the scientists for the major controversy that was to come three years later. In 1924 Raymond Dart, professor of anatomy at Witwatersrand University in South Africa, dug up a skull and face bone of a hominid. He announced that the remains had belonged to a six-year-old child whose milk teeth had already appeared. Early in February of 1925 he published a paper about his discovery, which he named *Australopithecus africanus*. He claimed that the small skull was some sort of being between a man and an ape. He was immediately greeted with scorn. Many of the most eminent prehistorians referred to it jokingly as "Dart's Baby" and as the "Taung Baby." They were sure it was a chimpanzee.

Some fossil experts did come to Dart's aid. An English paleontologist, Dr. Robert Broom, hurried to Johannesburg to examine the Taung skull. He pointed out that the child-ape had no resemblance to any living anthropoids such as the gorilla and chimpanzee. It did resemble man. After he wrote a paper declaring the creature to be the "missing link," he managed to enlist the support of William J. Sollas, the noted Oxford paleontologist. But their minority opinion couldn't prevail against the larger group of scientists who still considered the find trivial. Meanwhile in Cambridge, a young undergraduate read about the relic with great interest; Louis Leakey wondered if Raymond Dart might not be right.

In the meantime, Louis wished to see more European relics. With the coming of the Christmas vacation when Louis was free to do more research, he visited the museums of Europe. The College Council gave him a generous grant and he crossed the Channel to visit exhibits in Hamburg, Brussels, and Berlin. It was in Berlin that he met Hans Reck. He was gratified to receive a warm welcome from the geologist he had read so much about. They quickly found common ground, for they both had been dinosaur fossil hunting in Tendaguru in Tanganyika. During the stay they became close friends and hoped one day to go on safari together to Oldoway (later called Olduvai), where Reck had found what he still considered a prehistoric skeleton. After studying the remains, Leakey was inclined to agree with him. The two men were mutually agreed that Africa might prove to contain the most important anthropological sites in the world.

After his return to Cambridge for the winter term, Louis prepared to get into the field. Influenced by his momentous meeting with Reck, he knew where he wanted to go. During the Easter vacation he began to make plans for an expedition to Kenya. He had until the end of the summer term to raise money for the venture. When the long-awaited graduation day came he received a degree in archaeology and anthropology. He was also awarded a research fellowship from St. John's College and a grant for his planned expedition.

A conversation he had with a professor shortly afterward wasn't encouraging. When the man found out that Leakey was going to Africa he laughed. He told the young graduate that he was throwing away a brilliant future by wasting his time there. If he was smart he would go to Asia. That was where the evidence was to be found. But Louis had had experience with advice from teachers. Mr. Conway at Weymouth College had suggested that he join a bank. As usual the young anthropologist ignored the warning and went his own way. If he were wrong, it would be his own time he had wasted.

Already he had in mind special sites to examine in areas where he had picked up pieces of obsidian after thunderstorms. The Kikuyu thought these to be *nyenji cia ngoma* ("razors of the spirits") hurled from a sacred mountaintop by the storm spirits. He had noted another fascinating factor while plotting on a map the spread of early hand-ax culture, which extended from India to Northern Europe, including the center of East Africa. He wondered if it had spread from the continent of his birth. Hadn't Darwin predicted that our early ancestors lived in the Dark Continent rather than anywhere else?

Thus in July of 1926, Louis Leakey bought third-class

steamship tickets to Mombasa for himself and his close friend Bernard H. Newsam, a talented geology student. They were members of the impressively titled East African Archaeological Expedition. They only hoped they could live up to it.

The Fossil Site
of Makalia

When Louis arrived in Kabete he selected the site of
Gibberish Cave, scene of his first childhood expedition,
for the excavations. As on that earlier day, he had to take
into account the imaginary world of Kikuyu superstition.
After hiring two local tribesmen to help him he ran into
labor trouble. The helpers were afraid to touch the bones
of a dead person, no matter how long the person had been
buried in the ground. According to tribal law, anyone
handling such human remains had to be purified in a strict
ceremony and then offer a sacrifice before entering his or
her home.

To avoid the tribal taboo, Leakey turned to those Kikuyus who had become Christians. Having given up the old
traditions they had no objection to digging for bones. One
mission convert, Ndekei, had been a childhood friend,
and he helped recruit other men for the crew. However,
even this enlightened group had to be convinced that their
predecessors had used the black stones for knives and
weapons. They had their own names for the obsidian
pieces. They still believed they were *nyenji cia ngoma,*
"razors of the spirits," or *nyura-nyura,* "divine
thunderbolts."

The workers insisted that these strange objects appeared from nowhere after heavy storms. Louis tried to explain that the stone flakes were buried in the ground and were exposed by rain washing away the earth. It was only after he had called attention to the phenomenon again and again that they believed him. Any doubt completely vanished when Louis took a piece of obsidian and showed them how Stone Age people might have trimmed the *nyura-nyura*. The Kikuyus all agreed that the black flakes made excellent knives for skinning goats.

After months of excavation no bones were found, and in October Leakey boarded a train with crew and equipment to move the project to Nakuru, a village a hundred miles away. Some years before, a Major MacDonald had notified the newspapers about a prehistoric site on his farm near Nakuru. Louis obtained permission from him to carry out fossil research there, and he hired a lorry to carry the camp equipment to the MacDonald farm.

Once they were settled, the major took Leakey to the slopes of a small lava cliff. Heavy boulders and rocks were piled against its steep face. Leaky conjectured that the blocks of stone might conceal the opening of a cave. MacDonald mentioned his theory that it could be a burying ground. But before they got to work there were practical considerations to take care of. There was no water at the site. MacDonald offered to let the party use an irrigation ditch he had built a mile away. It meant continuous hikes to and from the camp, and Louis pitched in with the local people to maintain a water supply for drinking and washing. In the course of setting up camp, Louis gained the respect of the local tribesmen, a fact that would be very important for the work that was to come.

Newsam adapted well to African life, although at one point he caused pandemonium among the local inhabitants. Somehow he had gotten himself one of the leather aprons usually worn by the Kikuyu women. While watching the natives dance one evening he produced his souvenir and handed it to a Kikuyu warrior. The man stared at it for a moment in amazement, and then the entire tribe of dancers fled in horror. Apparently there were serious penalties for a man touching a leather apron.

Leakey couldn't afford to break any tribal taboos, accidentally or not. The crew was already far too small for the amount of work to be done at the site. He therefore engaged a laborer from the nearby village, Juma Gitau, who became a talented excavator.

At Nakuru, Leakey and Newsam explored the countryside in an old Model T Ford. They wanted to study the geology of the area to determine what climatic conditions had existed in ancient times. One day in January of 1927, the two men were walking along the shores of Lake Nakuru. Leakey commented that he expected to find prehistoric remains in the Rift Valley because Stone Age people had to live close to water to survive.

Newsam added that the geology of the area had changed radically since then. He explained that the shore of the lake thousands of years before was probably as much as 145 feet higher than at present. That meant that the Nakuru site, now a considerable distance from the water, had been only a few hundred yards away in the prehistoric era. The variation was due to changes in climate over thousands of years.

These discussions led to the search for another site on a farm at the south end of Lake Nakuru. In a district called Elmenteita, the owner had cut away a section of cliff for a water course. In the process he had exposed some human skulls. Leakey and Newsam started excavating and found a skull jutting out of a pocket of silt in the face of the cliff.

They were even more delighted when they later discovered a second skull in almost perfect condition.

Since the site could prove important, Leakey got in touch with a Mr. Gamble, the brother-in-law of the man who owned the property. Gamble gave the two scientists permission to set up the Elmenteita camp in a large shed with a waterproof thatched roof, two bedrooms, a living room, kitchen, and storage area. It was far more comfortable than the usual tents. The Makalia River, meandering down from the high hills, supplied water for their living needs and for the radiator of the old Ford.

The valley of Makalia was rich in human skulls and skeletons. It seemed that a Stone Age community had buried its dead along the edge of a low cliff by the river. Fortunately the burial site had been covered over by lake silt rich in mineral salts. Thus the fossils were well preserved. Besides a wealth of tools and bones at Makalia, there were "hundreds of pottery fragments." The art of making pots signified that the people lived in the late Stone Age. But the fossils from Elmenteita appeared to be older than those dug up at Lake Nakuru.

One day while playing tennis with Leakey at the farm, Gamble told him that there were also some caves on his land. After finishing work at the Makalia site, Louis had time to inspect two rock shelters halfway up a steep hill. They looked as if they might have been a likely place for prehistoric people to make their homes. He started work on the rich site at Gamble's Cave in April. But after several months Leakey had to halt the excavation. It was obvious that to properly explore the area would take a great deal of time. Regretfully, he was coming to the end of his expedition. He had to return to Cambridge for graduate work and to raise more money for a second trip.

As he prepared for the voyage to England, Leakey

experienced doubt about what he had accomplished. He wasn't certain that he could convince the experts that he had made a significant start in prehistoric research. If they judged his work useless he would never be able to get another grant to continue exploration. On the other hand, he had achieved more than he had expected. With Newsam, he packed 106 crates of fossil specimens and loaded them on the train for the 300-mile trip to Mombasa, where they would be transferred to a steamer.

Before leaving for England in July of 1927, Leakey asked one of his native workers to take charge of the camp at Makalia. Juma Gitau, a Kikuyu who had converted to Islam, had been of invaluable help during their stay. He had quickly become as competent at excavation as his two better educated colleagues. Louis gave the experienced worker shellac and plaster to preserve any fossils he might find while they were gone. He was not surprised when he arrived in Cambridge to receive a letter from Gitau. Included was a picture of a human skeleton he had dug up at Elmenteita. Leakey was anxious to get back.

During the winter of 1927 Louis traveled to Munich to examine the famous skeleton discovered by Hans Reck. In the light of his own work in Kenya, he came to the conclusion that the skulls from Elmenteita closely resembled the remains of Olduvai Gorge. He also became convinced of something else. None of these bones could possibly be from the ancestors of Masai tribesmen. They were much older.

When he returned to Cambridge, paleontologists were excited about another discovery that seemed to prove that Asia was the birthplace of the human race. While still an undergraduate, Louis had read of an exploration by a young scientist in 1921 on Dragon Bone Hill near the Chinese village of Chou Kou Tien. That scientist's discovery of two human molars from the Pleistocene period had led to a second expedition in 1927, under Davidson Black, a young Canadian anatomist.

The project, well equipped and sponsored by the Rockefeller Foundation, had found a hominid tooth in the same village south of Peking. This was enough of a find, for teeth are distinctive. A paleontologist can tell from what animal a tooth comes. In an article that appeared in the prestigious British journal *Nature,* in November of 1927, Black revealed that on the basis of this single molar a new genus of man was proposed. It took its place with *Pithecanthropus erectus, (Homo erectus),* the type Dubois had found thirty years earlier in Java. Named *Sinanthropus pekinensis,* or Peking man, it was at the time accepted as another example of the "missing link." Today it is considered to be *Homo erectus.*

Still, against this almost overwhelming evidence, Leakey believed that the true original of man would be found in Africa. He was encouraged in this idea by his teacher, Arthur Keith. Under the influence of the great anatomist, Louis learned a great deal about the construction and development of the human body. Keith also helped him plan a second expedition to Africa. He got further assistance in financing the venture from his old friend, Dr. Haddon.

At the end of his year of residence at Cambridge, Leakey began to look for able students of prehistory to join him in the fossil search. One with whom he shared a great love of birds, Donald MacInnes, was a promising graduate student at Trinity College. When MacInnes visited Louis in his workroom he brought some skull fragments that didn't look like they could possibly be reconstructed. They were of Saxon or Roman date and had been dug up near Cambridge. The next time Louis saw them they had been fitted together to form complete skulls. He was astonished at MacInnes's knowledge and skill and asked him to join the expedition. The young man accepted enthusiastically.

Another student, Wilfrida Avern, agreed to accompany the party as more than a colleague. She and Louis were married shortly before the expedition embarked for Africa. Engaged during the spring, they decided to celebrate the coming trip by having the wedding in Cambridge before they left.

Kikuyu warriors stand in front of the Leakey home in Kabete in 1903. A workman on the roof renews thatch on the veranda.

Louis Leakey on a dinosaur dig in Tanganyika in 1924.

Mary Leakey and crew look for precious bits of a skull trampled by the Masai tribes' cattle.

The Dinotherium provided a gigantic windfall for Chellean man at Olduvai.

OLDUVAI GORGE

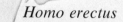

Homo erectus

"Cinderella"

"George"

Zinjanthropus

Homo habilis
child

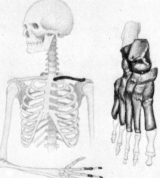

Homo habilis
woman

Stone Circle

Olduvai Gorge in Tanzania contains one of the richest deposits of prehistoric fossils ever discovered. Here Louis S. B. Leakey discovered the remains and tools of creatures who lived two million years ago. A beach umbrella protects Dr. Leakey, his wife Mary, and son Philip from the searing sun. The dalmatians and a fox terrier guard them against snakes and wild animals.

Richard and Meave Leakey and African staff swaying on camels at Lake Turkhana.

Stone-ax storehouse shows wares manufactured 200,000 years ago. A near-fatal step in 1929 led Dr. Leakey to the first known living site of hand-ax man. At Kariandusi, Kenya, he shows Mrs. Melvin Bell Grosvenor where he almost stumbled over a cliff and clutched at bushes to save himself.

Louis Leakey bakes "beautifully baked bread" at Olduvai.

*Richard Leakey chats
with the Masai at
Olduvai Gorge.*

*Jonathan Leakey and
son at the snake farm
in northern Kenya.*

Danger on a Cliff

Louis Leakey stopped long enough in Kabete to introduce his pretty wife to his family. Although it was a pleasant visit, he was anxious to get to work at Elmenteita. His brother, Douglas, who had been studying geography at Cambridge, had already sailed from England to set up the camp. When the Leakeys arrived at the site they discovered that Douglas had repaired the roof of a dilapidated farmhouse and restored the rooms. There was a living and dining room and three bedrooms. It would provide ample lodgings for the newlyweds, MacInnes, and a Miss Elizabeth Kitson and Mrs. Ciceley Creasey who were to arrive later from England. For a touch of luxury the crew installed a zinc bathtub. Compared to the hut Louis had shared with Newsam, the farmhouse was sumptuous.

The first thing Leakey did after settling accommodations was to hurry to the prehistoric burial site at Makalia to examine the place where Juma Gitau had excavated a skeleton. It turned out to be an important relic, and he told his friend he was sure more would be found. He went to Makalia and left the digging there in the charge of Powys Cobb, a Cambridge undergraduate who had paid his own way to participate in the project. Louis and his wife continued to the excavations at Gamble's Cave, a rich storehouse filled with thousands of obsidian blades and scrapers.

Meanwhile, Donald MacInnes set out on his own in the Elmenteita district to search for fossils exposed in the ancient lake deposits. While trying to ascertain details of the cliff formation, he found a number of animal bones and then, while looking further, saw human bones sticking out of the side of a low cliff. He reported them to Leakey and the digging at Gamble's Cave was stopped. The whole party joined MacInnes. This decision was almost to cost two of its members their lives.

In November, Leakey and MacInnes were excavating at Donald's new site and discovered a human skull deeply embedded in the face of the cliff. Lying on their sides, cramped in a narrow crevice, they laboriously worked their small knives into the rock. It was too hard, and after hours of effort they considered blasting the skull free. But the blast might shatter the fossil and could bring the top of the cliff crashing down on them. They decided against it.

Finally they managed to cut the skull loose, and while MacInnes continued to work, Leakey carried the relic down to the party below. Powys Cobb offered to relieve Leakey, and as he went off to join MacInnes, the expedition leader warned him to be careful. If he dug too deep the whole cliff could come toppling down on him. But the warning had come too late. No sooner had Cobb started digging than there was a tremendous roar and, as the others watched horrified, the cliff thundered down on the two men.

Leakey thought they were dead. With the help of the Kikuyu workmen he feverishly tore away the pile of rock and soil. When MacInnes and Cobb were pulled free they were, miraculously, still alive. The excavating that had led to the catastrophe had also saved them. They had been chipping away at a small cave, the weak point of the cliff, and their bodies had been far enough inside to be protected from the avalanche. Although their legs were badly bruised and cut and they were considerably shaken, they were all right after a few minutes.

A Kikuyu had a different explanation for the incident. He pointed a finger accusingly at Leakey and said that the accident was caused by the spirit of the man whose skull had been taken from the rock. Louis knew the Kikuyu was wrong, but Louis also knew that he himself was responsible. He should have stopped the digging at that spot after they removed the skull, and shouldn't have let Cobb go up there. But the young scientist had been carried away by the excitement of their find. He was determined in the future to put the safety of his workers above everything else.

The following Sunday, Leakey tried to restore some humor to the camp. He was scheduled to pick up the new staff members, Miss Elizabeth Kitson and Mrs. Ciceley Creasey, at the railroad station in Elmenteita. He knew they would be apprehensive about their first trip to wild Africa, and he didn't want to disappoint them. To introduce his new staff members to the dangers of the Dark Continent, he staged a fitting welcome.

Toward the end of the drive back to camp they had to travel across a flat treeless plain and pass through a desolate place. To scare the women Leakey called it Lion's Corner. Leakey had told the two women that when the predatory lions were unable to find food they often rested there. As they reached the spot a terrifying roar came out of the brush. Then moving closer, another and another. The women turned white and shrank in their seats.

"They're after us," Louis shouted, and stepped on the gas. Miss Kitson and Mrs. Creasey were too frightened to look back.

That night at supper the women recounted their narrow escape. Frida Leakey, knowing her husband's enjoyment of practical jokes, cornered him in the kitchen afterward. She wanted to know how he had gotten the lions to roar at exactly the right time.

Leakey laughed and explained the hair-raising sound. He had stationed some Kikuyu in the bush and when they saw the car coming they started to roar. He admitted that the growling was so perfect that, had he not spent most of his life in Africa, he would have been frightened too.

But the snake that greeted the newcomers in their room that night was no hoax. Miss Kitson was ready to go back to England when she saw the long black reptile lying motionless on the floor. Frida came running in and when she saw the snake was about to call Louis. But then she hesitated. It might be another of his practical jokes. It was probably dead. She cautiously stepped closer for a better look when it moved. She screamed for her husband, and he came charging in with his rifle cocked. It wasn't a joke, and he killed the snake with a single shot. A few days later John Solomon, an English geologist who had joined the expedition, also encountered a snake and only at the last minute managed to sidestep it. Louis casually told the new members that puff adders seemed to be especially active that year.

In December, while working in Gamble's Cave, the group of young scientists discovered an entire human skeleton. Since the fossil looked as though it might be important, Leakey decided not to disinter the bones separately. Instead he set to work digging out the block of hard material in which it was buried. The entire block could then be sent intact to England where the delicate process of removing the bones could be done more easily. The task of chipping away at the matrix was very slow and difficult. In a cavity fourteen feet below the floor of the cave, Leakey patiently dug with small dental picks so as not to damage the fragile specimen.

A reporter on the scene excitedly cabled the news of the find to the English press. By this time the British public was aware of the fascinating work being done by Louis's expedition, and was eager for whatever news it could get. Unfortunately the reporter was more impressed with the method of excavation than with the relic itself, for weeks later a newspaper arrived with the headline, "Mr. Leakey discovers the first dentist. Fossil man found with dental picks." In fact the skeleton was important. It dated from a period earlier than anything Leakey had previously found in Kenya. At the time, it seemed to be comparable in age to many of the Cro-Magnon fossils already found in France and thus showed the wide distribution of early *Homo sapiens*. It also established that Africa was a fertile ground for prehistoric investigation.

The next months brought a number of frustrating problems that made further work more difficult. In January of 1929, there was a long period of drought. Every drop of water needed at Lion Hill, a rock shelter fifteen miles from Gamble's Cave, had to be brought by truck or on foot from a great distance away. At *Kampiya Giko,* "Dirty Camp," there was barely enough water to drink, let alone wash with, and the crew worked day after day in the broiling sun caked with dust and sweat.

Toward the end of April it finally rained, but this only made things worse. On the way to Lake Baringo, north of

Nakuru, the truck Leakey was driving became stuck in mud up to its axles. In the driving rain the crew managed to drag it free. When they reached the other side of the riverbed they set up camp. Canvas awnings were attached to the sides of the truck to serve as makeshift tents. Miss Kitson and Miss Jenkins slept under the awnings, and Leakey and his wife tried to make themselves comfortable on the floor of the truck. An hour later, soaked to the skin, the two women climbed into the truck to escape the downpour. But in the darkness they couldn't see what they were doing and with a tremendous crash they fell head first on top of the Leakeys, frightening them. After making sure that they hadn't been joined by two lions, Louis and Frida made room for their bedraggled guests. The four people spent a sleepless night talking and shivering cramped together in the damp compartment without an inch to spare.

When the weather finally cleared, the party went back to work at Gamble's Cave. They began excavating a deposit dating from about the time of the Aurignacian culture some 40,000 years ago. They were surprised to find pieces of pottery because, according to what was known of this stage of human development, humans hadn't yet discovered the use of clay. Louis was exultant for he believed he now had proof that ceramic work dated back as far as the Paleolithic era.

However, skeptics in England refused to accept his conclusions. Prehistory experts wrote to him that he had made a serious mistake and should withdraw his claim immediately. But Leakey stubbornly refused. He was certain he would find further evidence to support his theory that clay was used during the Aurignacian period. Unfortunately as he continued to explore the site he became increasingly discouraged. Although he found many tools and bones, the age of the layers couldn't be accurately determined. What he didn't know was that support of the antiquity of the pottery was to come from a visiting archaeologist in a matter of weeks.

Miss Elizabeth Kitson and John Solomon located on the Kariandisi River, near the village of Nakuru just below the equator, some dry lake beds that had been dislocated by faults in the Great Rift valley. Erosion had uncovered archaeological sites. They dug up hand axes that gave Leakey the evidence he needed. The implements belonged to a culture that was in existence for millions of years, during the time when the great crack of the Rift was being formed in the earth's surface. The sediments containing the tools could be dated. Louis prepared to attend a meeting of the British Association for the Advancement of Science in Johannesburg, South Africa, to present a paper offering his evidence for the existence of an early hand-ax culture.

On June 13, 1929, he began the journey to Johannesburg. When the group started out they knew they were in for a hard trip. They traveled over almost impassable roads at the end of the rainy season. His wife, John Solomon, and Elizabeth Kitson took turns driving. Jannai Kigamba, a truck mechanic, went along in case of trouble on the primitive Great North Road that ran from Cairo to the Cape of Good Hope. There were few hotels of any sort along the way.

Farther south they stopped briefly at Broken Hill in Northern Rhodesia (now Zambia) to visit an ancient mine where in 1921 a fossil skull had been found by Zwiglar, a Swiss worker. Zwiglar, still employed there, guided Leakey to the deposits where he spent some time collecting a few cases of prehistoric relics from the mining dumps. Then the heavily loaded ton-and-a-half Chevrolet pickup jolted over the rough roads of the granite mountains and down into precipitous rock gulleys. If the truck went too fast, there was the danger of breaking the back axle. If it went too slowly, it became stuck in the sand. The group frequently had to dig it out and by jacking up the rear wheels with branches got it moving again. A smashed back spring had to be replaced at a small town called Wankie. Truck parts were in short supply in Central Africa.

Along the way they passed through lion country. Leakey was anxious to show his wife her first African lion. Rounding a curve he saw in the distance what looked like seven of the beasts hiding in the tall grass. Excitedly he handed the field glasses to Wilfrida and she scanned the bush for a sight of the magnificent animals. Finally she handed the glass back and broke into laughter. When Leakey had focused on the group he saw seven donkeys standing dumbly watching the truck rumble by. He sheepishly admitted that he was perhaps a better prehistorian than wildlife guide.

After six weeks on the road the party arrived for the scientific conference in Johannesburg. In the midst of the formal academic atmosphere, Leakey's contribution was a breath of fresh air. No longer awed by an audience of scholars, Louis gave an enthusiastic presentation of his finds in East Africa. The members were so fascinated with his findings that a number of them decided to travel to Kenya to see the fossil relics and cultural artifacts on their way home.

To make preparations for their visit—the scientists would arrive in groups of sixteen at a time—Leakey had only fifteen days to make the return journey of 3,000 miles. It was the frantic trip from Lindi to Dar es Salaam all over again. But this time Louis wasn't returning as a student to the university. He was driving over the roads and highways of his native Africa to receive his colleagues as a scientist whose knowledge and work were beginning to be fully recognized.

The Skeleton
from Gamble's Cave

Once back in Nairobi the young host had scarcely two days to check the extensive plans being made for the three hundred visiting scholars. He had to provide railway transportation, arrange for lodging accommodations, and contact local settlers who would be able to drive the scientists the twenty-eight miles to the sites at Elmenteita. In addition, he had to reopen the prehistoric sites. Gamble's Cave had been boarded up to discourage the increasing number of tourists who had heard about it and were intent on hunting for Stone Age relics themselves.

After he had welcomed the first party of sixteen, Louis took them to the exposed entrance to Gamble's Cave. Thirty feet below the level of the cave floor he had dug up another rich deposit of bones and hand tools. The group was astounded at the enormous number of stone knives and blade scrapers that had been unearthed there in the previous eight months. Leakey told them that he had found literally thousands of these obsidian implements and even invited each of them to take home a prehistoric tool as a souvenir.

The men of science did just that and then marched over to the verandah where Wilfrida Leakey had prepared a large lunch. Sitting at the long wooden table, one of the scholars, a professor of agriculture, held up a piece of sharpened obsidian. "I'm going to use this to cut my meat," he announced, and then he easily sliced the *nyama* with a knife that Leakey told him had been fashioned at least 20,000 years before.

A distinguished archaeologist, Professor Fleure, arrived in a later party and was especially intrigued by the pottery Leakey had found. Previously these relics of an ancient culture had been generally discounted by the scientific community. Fleure agreed with Leakey that they indeed dated from the Paleolithic period. On a digging expedition with the respected scientist, Leakey had a bit of luck. The two men found another fine fragment of the same pottery in its original location. Fleure was now convinced that the first clay work did go as far back as the Aurignacian period, and Leakey was gratified to have an unbiased expert support his controversial view. Today, however, most scientists do not think that the pottery was made at that time. They think that the pieces that Louis found had come from a disturbed context, where later artifacts were muddled up with earlier ones.

Fleure spent another few days in the camp so that Louis could show him some promising sites in the area of Lake Naivasha. After lunch with the governor of Nairobi, they returned in time to greet another party of scientists, among them such eminent men in archeology and geology as J. L. Myers, P. G. H. Boswell, and George D. Balfour. Neither would they forget the hectic schedule after they jumped into an expedition car at Nairobi. Leakey put them through their academic paces in a whirlwind tour over hundreds of miles in the Kenya highland. In the daytime they inspected sites of the Lake Nakuru basin, and evenings found them pouring over Leakey's prehistoric specimens. On the final day, they barely reached Nairobi in time to board the train for Mombasa. One of the scientists said it for all, "This has been the most strenuous two days I have ever spent, and what's more, I will never forget what I've seen here."

Back in camp, Louis received a telegram from the governor asking him to come to Nairobi immediately. It was an urgent matter concerning the Kikuyu. Sir Edward Gregg had appointed him a member of a special committee to investigate the native system of land tenure. Since it was already past noon, he didn't even have time to change out of his bush clothes. Frida quickly packed a suitcase for the hundred-mile trip to the Kenyan capital. They jumped into the pickup truck, the only vehicle available, and started out for Nairobi.

It was almost dusk when Leakey pulled up to the main entrance of Government House. A sentry immaculately attired in a crisp khaki uniform and red fez took one look at his creased, soiled clothes and demanded to know what he wanted. At first he didn't believe Leakey when he said that he had been asked to come by the governor. Finally a government official recognized the young couple and invited them inside.

Leakey parked the mud-encrusted truck among the fleet of limousines and they hurried up the steps of the magnificent marble mansion. A porter took their bag and led them to their room. They stood a moment amazed at the opulence of the elegantly furnished suite. Getting ready to clean up, Leakey observed that it would be a sacrilege to take the dirt of Gamble's Cave into the spotless porcelain bathroom. While he was enjoying a marvelously hot bath, there was a knock at the door. When Frida opened it there was an aide-de-camp standing stiffly at attention in the hall. "His Excellency," the man announced importantly, "prefers dinner jackets and no decorations, no tails." That was just fine for all Leakey owned in evening attire was the jacket.

After an elaborate dinner in the state dining room, the special committee went into a private study to conduct business. Besides the government officials and committee members, there were present a number of Kikuyu elders. The problem they presented was the same that had existed since the first English settlers arrived in East Africa. The Africans were being forced off their land. They feared that even more territory would be taken from them, and that they would lose valuable pastureland needed for their livestock. Since Louis was the only European present who spoke fluent Kikuyu, he was called on both as a translator and an advisor to the tribesmen. He was also one of the only officials they trusted.

By the time the committee investigations were over, it was time to go back to Cambridge. While in Kenya, Leakey had been elected to a research fellowship at St. John's College. Now that he was married he could move into a comfortable cottage outside the town. This solved what was becoming a major problem. The three rooms that he had occupied at St. John's could now be used to store the sixty new cases of prehistoric tools he had gathered during 1926–1927. The human bones and animal remains could be shipped as usual to the Royal College of Surgeons and to the British Museum of Natural History.

When Leakey returned to London he faced the difficult and delicate task of removing the Gamble's Cave skeleton from its rocklike matrix and putting the bones together. Through the weeks of exhausting labor he was greatly helped by his previous companion, Donald MacInnes, who was now a student of vertebrate zoology at London University. After they had freed the skull, jaw, and some limbs from the stubborn matrix, Leakey again noticed the strong resemblance between the Gamble's Cave specimen and the skull unearthed at Olduvai Gorge by Hans Reck.

Now Leakey was anxious to discuss his find with the famous geologist. Reck had claimed a greater age for his discovery than Leakey was able to assign to his Gamble's Cave skeleton. So he decided to make a trip to Berlin to resolve the problem of dating both fossil skulls. In effect, Louis believed that the other scientist had been mistaken about the age of his relic.

Not surprisingly, the meeting of the two prehistorians resulted in a hotly contested debate. Louis emphasized that the fossil deposits at Olduvai Gorge were probably of the same age as the beds where Elizabeth Kitson and John Solomon had unearthed the hand-ax culture. On that premise he was sure that there must be stone implements of the same culture at Olduvai. He was convinced that if early humans once lived by an ancient lake as Reck's specimen had done from the evidence of associated fossils then there had to be stone tools as well.

The continued disagreement ended with Leakey's suggestion that his friend join the third expedition he was planning to East Africa. Even though Reck welcomed the chance to prove his young colleague wrong, he had his doubts about the project. He tried to discourage Louis from what seemed a hopeless venture. He insisted that he had already combed the area and had discovered only fossil bones.

But the exceptionally strong-willed Leakey was not to be so easily persuaded. He pointed out that Reck had only explored the gorge once. Leakey fully expected to excavate Olduvai and find a place where primitive tools had been made. He was even so brash as to bet that he would uncover stone implements within twenty-four hours of their arrival at the site.

Back in England during the spring of 1931, Louis had another assignment as interpreter for a Kikuyu chief being entertained at Cambridge. Chief Koinange was in Great Britain to consult with a joint committee of both Houses of Parliament on the question of a closer union between the British territories in Africa, including Kenya. In the course of the discussions, he had a few words to say about the young man who had been born in his country. "We call Louis the black man with the white face," he said, "because he is more African than European. In all ways we regard him as one of ourselves." Leakey considered it as great a compliment as any he had received from the scientific community.

When his duties as diplomat were over, he completed the final plans for the expedition to Olduvai. He had received generous grants from the Royal Geographic Society and the Percy Sladen Memorial Trust and was delighted to learn that Dr. A. T. Hopwood, an outstanding paleontologist, had been appointed by the British Museum to accompany him in the field. He was somewhat disappointed to lose the services of the Abbé Breuil, a world-famous French prehistorian he had hoped to enlist for the expedition. Breuil had already made plans to go to China to work with Dr. Davidson Black, who had discovered two human teeth on Dragonbone Hill near Choukoutien in 1927. Said to be of the same age as *Pithecanthropus*, the remains belonged to the species of Peking man identified earlier by Eugène Dubois.

Having recruited an extensive expeditionary staff, Louis arrived in Kenya in June of 1931. He drove to Limuru, a suburb of Nairobi where his parents had retired from the mission in Kabete. They gave him a plot of land for a three-room bungalow, which he built with the aid of eight Kikuyu workmen. While he was away from what would be the base camp at Limuru, the hut with mud and wattle walls and a corrugated tin roof would house his wife and newborn baby daughter, Priscilla. He also took this period to recruit a well-known hunter and guide to protect the party from the lions and rhinoceros that inhabited the territory around Olduvai. He sent Captain J. H. Hewlett, who had escorted the Prince of Wales on his African safaris, to map out a route for the expedition over the treacherous dirt tracks that wound down steep gullies and through the wild bush country.

A few days before the arrival of the party, Leakey had everything ready for the coming expedition with Reck. He decided to spend the time driving the sixty miles from Kabete to the Kariandusi site where the hand-axes had been uncovered by Solomon and Kitson. He had always wanted to take a close look at this excavation area in the Rift Valley. Parking his lorry, he started out with his Kikuyu guides to tramp through the heavily wooded brush. Some time later he came to the edge of a canyon and peered over in absolute amazement. There, stuck in the face of the cliff, were dozens of prehistoric tools. In his excitement he nearly lost his balance. As he toppled over the edge he frantically clutched at some bushes and only at the last instant saved himself from falling fifty feet down a vertical precipice. When he had sat down and pulled himself together he turned and peered over the rocky ledge that had almost cost him his life. What he saw took his breath away. There below were over a thousand black stone tools scattered in the valley at his feet. It was a vast storehouse of human implements then thought to be at least 20,000 years old, and much older than ever found before. With considerable regret he left the site and went back to Limuru to wait for Reck, Hopwood, and Hewlett.

On September 22 the full expedition left the base camp for the three hundred mile trip to Olduvai. In addition to one car, there were three ton-and-a-half pickups to carry the heavy equipment and food supplies. Hans Reck, skeptical about the whole thing from the start, didn't think the trucks would make it. The overloaded trucks would have to negotiate the extremely rough roadless terrain. After looking at Hewlett's maps, Reck didn't even believe they would end up at the gorge. As confident as ever, Leakey was sure his vehicles would make it.

Reck's fears became even greater when the safari began its dangerous descent down the sheer rock cliffs of the Kikuyu Escarpment. He expected on every foot of the way that the trucks would careen over the edge and plummet into the gorge below. When they got to the bottom, there were new problems. The lush grassland appeared level and solid and perfectly safe. But beneath the heavy brush the ground was split with crevices and covered with rocks. The caravan could only average about five miles an hour. One reason for the slow pace was the frequent halts to cool the engines. The African drivers couldn't go into top gear over rough terrain, and grinding along in second gear overheated the radiators. Four gallons of water were needed for every fifteen miles as they crossed over into Tanganyika. This caused a tremendous drain on the valuable water supply, and they were forced to use pools of rainwater where they could find them. The pools were brackish, filled with dirt and vegetation, and even after being filtered they clogged the engines.

Finally, after seven days of bone-jarring travel, the party reached Olduvai Gorge. The gorge was a mile wide and 300 feet deep, and pink castle towers of stone rose from the floor below. It was breathtaking. The walls of the canyon were sharply faulted and lifted, and the many colored layers of rock looked like slices from an enormous cake. Reck, as relieved that he had made it as he was delighted at the scene, jumped out of the lead car. Leakey graciously gave him the honor of being the first to stand on the banks of Olduvai.

Leakey and Hopwood had the job of finding a suitable place to pitch camp. There were two concerns. The Masailand, then part of the vast Serengeti Plains, was the hunting ground of a great number of game-stalking lions. The other problem was water. The area was exceptionally dry. When Louis mentioned this to Reck, the German told him not to worry. When he had been there before he had found a large waterhole. It would satisfy their needs for some time. The two men went off to find it, and when they reached the spot Reck once again experienced the harshness of the African countryside. He was amazed that the pool had dried up. Then he remembered that some of his workmen had located a small spring on the slopes of the Ngorongoro Crater about thirteen miles away. He and Hopwood took five-gallon cans and a truck and set out to get water.

After they'd left, Leakey took a Kikuyu helper back to the dry hole to dig deeper in hopes of finding even a trace of water. On the way he kept an eye out for artifacts. He was delighted when his companion found a perfectly shaped hand-ax. Recognizing it immediately as Acheulean (an early Stone Age period), he could hardly wait for Reck to get back to show it to him. He had won his bet. He had found a stone tool within eight hours. But the party didn't return. By dark Louis began to get worried. After supper he took some porters to the outskirts of the camp and set up torches to serve as landmarks in case Reck and Hopwood had gotten lost in the bush.

By midnight they still hadn't appeared. From his tent he could see the animals starting to gather. He counted twenty pairs of hyena eyes in the darkness. He decided to look for the missing men. After a fruitless four-mile drive with Hewlett he finally gave up. He fervently hoped that their delay was caused by nothing more serious than a flat tire. But still, remembering the incident with Cobb and MacInnes, he was angry at himself for not sending Hewlett with them. Neither of the two men was a good shot.

Exhausted with the day and worn out with worrying about the missing men, he dozed fitfully outside his tent. When he heard a noise he started awake, thinking it might be them. But it was only the sounds of the African night. Finally, in the early hours of morning, he was relieved to hear the truck and see the headlights probing their way toward the camp. When he asked Reck what had happened, the scientist was surprised at his anxiety. They had filled the cans at Langavata Spring and, since it was late and they didn't know the terrain, decided to sleep in the truck. They hadn't bothered to light a signal fire because they hadn't thought that Leakey would go out on a wild goose chase looking for them. Reck, apparently, hadn't seen any danger in sleeping unguarded in the open.

At dawn Louis went back to the prehistoric tool site at the old water hole. Before long he found a second ax, this time in its original rock matrix. It indicated that Acheulean man had once inhabited the plains through which the gorge now cuts. When he showed the implement to Reck, the geologist was amazed that there was indeed a stone tool of great antiquity. Reck also admitted that he had been wrong about the absence of tools. Leakey's Gamble's Cave skeleton, as proved later, was of much the same age as Reck's specimen.

Leakey had to take a very sick Kikuyu worker back to Nairobi, and thus it wasn't until October 10 that he was able to pick up MacInnes and bring him back to Olduvai. They both agreed that the gorge had been worth waiting for. Over a period of months working more on knees than on feet, they unearthed a rich deposit of Stone Age relics, which were embedded at every level of the gorge. They determined that the sediments of which the layers were composed had been laid in and around a former lake. The staff then got down to the long, slow business of analyzing its find. They believed that there had been an orderly progress in the evolution of the hand-ax culture and that by arranging the stone implements in chronological order, they were able to chart prehistoric man's growing sophistication in the use of tools. It was a major achievement for Louis Leakey. The twenty-eight-year-old anthropologist had organized and led an expedition that revealed one of the oldest cultures found anywhere in the world.

The work at Olduvai Gorge was beset with discomfort and serious dangers. Hewlett was forced to kill two lions who attacked the group while they were bathing in a stream. A wounded rhinoceros with a festering gash in his side from an old gunshot wound charged Leakey from a distance of ten yards. Louis barely had time to grab his rifle and, after momentarily side-stepping the enraged beast, wheeled and dropped the huge animal with a well-aimed shot. Had he glanced up a second later he would have been killed.

The safari party also faced the blazing heat of the African sun and a constant wind that blew fine dust over everything. They were continually covered with dust, and the food they ate was gritty with dirt. There was never enough water. The cans had to be refilled almost daily, and after a few hours in the heat the water became foul and metallic. Nevertheless, the two-month expedition was a success. Leakey sent over a hundred crates of tools to Nairobi and packed cases of fossil bones for shipment to the British Museum in London. Even with this, the scientists had only scratched the surface. They marked out sites for future exploration in the incredibly rich beds of the prehistoric gorge, such as the Frida Leakey Korongo, a water channel named for his wife.

What with stone implements cropping up in every level of the gorge, this aspect of the prehistoric paradise proved to be of great significance. There were five geological beds at Olduvai with the first four consisting of old lake deposits of early and Middle Pleistocene times. After working from Bed I to Bed V, Louis had unearthed a full sequence of hand-ax culture. Up to now only isolated occurrences of hand-axes had been dug up in France, England, and Germany mostly in disturbed contexts such as gravel pits. But Leakey had found undisturbed campsites with stone tools and bone food refuse in close proximity to each other so that their relative age could be determined. At Olduvai, the ancient lake and landscape had been gradually covered by distinct layers of sediment and volcanic ash. In subsequent periods, earth movements caused by volcanic activity created faulting in the rocks so that it was not easy to identify the strata in which the sites occurred. Sometimes the fossils of certain extinct animals helped to identify the geological beds. In 1913 Professor Reck had dug up the remains of a *Dinotherium,* a strange cousin of the elephant.

The trip back to Limuru was even more difficult than the journey to Olduvai months before. The trucks began to fall apart, and the group was short on spare parts. On the last lap, heavy storms made the ground a sea of mud. The vehicles skidded from side to side, crashing into rocks and underbrush. The stalled trucks had to be pushed and dragged in the mire, and it was often impossible to get them started. At last, struggling up the slippery roads of the Kikuyu Escarpment, the party arrived at their base camp covered with mud and completely exhausted.

After the members of the expedition had left, Leakey set to work sorting out the material (stone) he had collected. One item particularly interested him. It was teeth from a prehistoric animal found in a deposit with some of the earliest stone tools. According to current paleontological beliefs, this animal had been extinct before stone tools were invented. The *Dinotherium,* a shaggy animal with short down-curving tusks, was supposed to have lived long before tool-making people came along. It seemed impossible that Acheulean man and this ancient creature had existed at the same time. The find seemed to indicate that tool-making people were around much longer ago than had been previously thought.

When Leakey announced his discovery of the fossil teeth and the flaked stone tools in the same rock deposit, the scientific community considered his claim absurd. Never one to be discouraged by such opposition, he decided to search for another fossil bed where further excavations might support his Olduvai find. He recalled that in 1913 Dr. Felix Oswald had collected some fossils much like his in the vicinity of Victoria Nyanza near Lake Victoria which adjoined both Uganda and Kenya. He organized another group, including Donald MacInnes, and in March of 1932 set out for the new site.

On the Kenya shore of the lake at a village called Kanjera he set up a camp. While digging for animal remains on a rain-drenched slope, MacInnes found fragments of three human skulls. Later, when pieced together, the skulls were said to belong to an early race of *Homo sapiens* who had lived in the Middle Pleistocene. Nearby were found Chellean hand-axes and animal fossils of the same prehistoric kind found in Bed II at Olduvai. But Leakey was intent on digging up more fossil deposits of *Dinotherium*.

On March 28, the expedition went to Kanam, four miles west of Kanjera where Juma Gitau, the head African assistant, dug up two *Dinotherium* teeth in a gully. Later, he broke up a lump of rock that yielded fossil teeth, but this time MacInnes recognized them as human. The teeth were the canine and the incisor (front), small and shaped like those of a modern human being, rather than large apelike teeth.

The fossil human jaw found by Gitau and encased in a rocky matrix (mass of material) required extensive study by Leakey. Later Leakey suggested that the Kanam mandible was "an ancestor and not a cousin of *Homo sapiens* who had lived in Africa in the Lower Pleistocene."

When Leakey published this information, his theory was met with skepticism. Doubtful scholars maintained that the Kanjera fossil had either been washed into an older deposit or the man to whom it belonged had died thousands of years later on the same spot as the *Dinotherium*. In any case Leakey's claim was too extreme to be taken seriously.

The discovery of the Kanam relic in many ways marked the end of a period in Leakey's life. Now thirty years old, he put aside forever the possibility of returning to Cambridge and settling down to a life of teaching. After the expedition at Kanjera and Kanam, he knew that he wanted to devote the rest of his life to anthropological work in the field. It was a turning point in another way as well. His marriage to Frida had been in a steady decline. After the birth of their second child, Colin, in 1933, they got a divorce.

As a result of the Kanam fossil, Leakey was becoming famous. When he published the third of many books, *The Stone Age Races of Kenya,* it was greeted with both enthusiasm and resentment. A number of his critics attributed his phenomenal success to sheer luck. To them he didn't seem to have done enough work to have earned his reputation. But Dr. Robert Broom made what was probably the truest comment about his achievement. "Leakey," he wrote, "with the restlessness of the true hunter, is always looking for something new, and with the intuition of true genius, generally looking in the right spot." His dissenters had missed the point. It was not that he had found it, but that he knew what it was.

A Windfall of
Hand-axes

It was at a dinner party that she almost missed that Mary
Douglas Nicol met Louis Leakey. The geology student
from London University had heard that there would be a
lecture, and it sounded dreadfully dull. But at the last
minute she decided to go anyway. Perhaps it would be
short.

When the handsome young man with the rakish mus-
tache stood up and began to speak, she realized that she
might be wrong. As Leakey described the excitement of
the expedition to Olduvai and the incredible significance
of the findings, his own passion for the subject began to
affect her. If he noticed the lovely young woman sitting in
the back row he gave no indication of it. Perhaps he
remembered the disastrous moment at Guild Hall when he
was momentarily distracted and forgot everything he had
to say.

But if he didn't notice her then, he certainly did afterward. They quickly became involved in an intense conversation about what turned out to be a shared interest. When
Louis learned that Mary Nicol had already done fieldwork, participating in a dig at a Stone Age site in England,
he asked her how she had become interested in prehis-

tory. She said that her father was a landscape painter and loved to sketch the countryside of southern France. She and her mother frequently went along. When she was eleven she had been taken to visit some ancient caves. A priest, Abbé Lémozi had shown her rock paintings done by early humans. She was so fascinated that he gave her books on the subject and taught her to excavate for fossils in the area. It was then that she had first decided to make prehistory her life work.

Over the next two years, while Louis was in graduate school at Cambridge, the couple saw each other quite often. They were brought even closer when Mary started illustrating the books Louis was preparing. After he received his Ph.D. he asked her to join the second expedition to Olduvai he was planning. She gladly accepted. During the months they spent together in East Africa the relationship quickly deepened, and they were married in December of 1935. Mary Leakey was to be far more than simply a wife. She was also to prove to be a considerably talented anthropologist.

She was already quite familiar with Louis's prehistoric finds. Together they read about another startling discovery that might shed further light on its origins. In the gravel beds of the Thames River in England, a Dr. Alvan T. Marston had dug up a number of fossils. He had found a human skull and Stone Age tools. This in itself wasn't unusual. Such objects had been found there before. But he also discovered, in the same deposits, the bones of an extinct elephantlike animal and a red deer that had lived in the warm climate of the Miocene era. At the time, Marston claimed that this Swanscombe fossil was the oldest human skull ever found in England.

Louis and Mary Leakey continued to believe that such evidence of human development as far back as the Miocene and Pliocene periods would be found in Africa. A discovery by a German scientist, Dr. Kohl Larsen, helped support their view. He had found in Tanganyika an extinct human type that caused a great deal of additional argument. Against powerful opposition, Leakey came to his aid in the book, *Adam's Ancestors*. He agreed with Larsen that the primitive hominid closely resembled the skulls of Java and Peking man and, like them, should be considered a species of *Pithecanthropus*.

In 1936 Dr. Robert Broom, now curator of the Transvaal Museum in Pretoria, joined the mounting controversy as an ally of Dart. On the basis of the position of the foramen magnum, an opening in the skull through which the spinal cord passes out of the brain, Dart had proposed that his *Australopithecus* walked upright. In humans the foramen magnum is at the base of the skull, which sits right on top of the neck and body. In four-legged animals the foramen magnum is more toward the back of the skull so the spinal cord can pass through a backbone that is more or less parallel to the ground rather than perpendicular to the ground, as in the case of humans who walk upright.

Dart and Broom did not have any pelvic or leg bones to uphold their proposal of the upright walk that the foramen magnum suggested. It was not until the late 1930s that Broom found the needed evidence. From two sites in South Africa he found enough bone fragments to piece together a few almost complete skulls. Most importantly, he found enough pelvic bone fragments to show that *Australopithecus* did indeed walk upright.

Despite the evidence that indicated an upright posture for *Australopithecus,* it was not at all clear whether this creature was a man or an ape. Dart and Broom could find no tools associated with the fossils. The geological circumstances in which Dart and Broom found the fossils made dating them extremely difficult. The finding of the fossils had occurred when blasting in quarrying operations uncovered ancient limestone caves.

Later, when he again explored the cave of Sterkfontein, Broom found the brain cast of another ape-man he called *Plesianthropus transvaalensis,* or near-man of Transvaal. In 1938, a few miles from Sterkfontein, Broom unearthed another ape-man, which he called *Paranthropus robustus,* or powerful near-man. Critics had a field day when Broom made the sensational claim that three different classes of apelike man—*Australopithecus* (southern ape-man), *Plesianthropus,* and *Paranthropus*—all once existed in the Transvaal. Skeptics refused to accept this ancestral link between man and ape. But other prehistorians, Leakey among them, were fascinated with the idea that three early forms of man might have lived in the same place.

In April of 1942 Louis obtained a three-day Easter pass and prepared to drive with hoarded gas rations to an area fifty miles southwest of Nairobi, near Mount Olorgesailie. Mary, always ready at a moment's notice to join an expedition, put Jonathan, born six weeks earlier, in safe hands and got ready for the trip. Although in a short time she had come to love Africa, she didn't enjoy seeing the packs of hyena they encountered on their way to Olorgesailie.

The Leakeys carefully explored the area. As they went deeper into the bush, the landscape became more eroded and cut by gullies. Over the ages volcanoes and earthquakes had lifted up part of a former lake basin and thus shaped the wild land so that torrential rains had been able to erode the beds and expose their contents. While Louis scoured one section in search of tools that might have been washed free, Mary worked a few hundred yards away.

After a few hours she heard her husband call out in excitement. He had found hundreds of hand-axes. She looked up and shouted back, "Louis, Louis, over here quickly."

When Louis hurried over he was staggered by what she'd discovered. There before them was a bonanza of axes, over three thousand of them. It seemed that Acheulean (early Stone Age) people had used this site to camp on the plains, in dry stream beds almost 400,000 years ago. Not only were there more tools than they had ever seen before, the implements were more advanced than any they had previously found. Stone Age man had designed and shaped them most carefully for use.

In addition to the hand-axes, the Leakeys found fossil bones of the animals who had once shared this land. Mount Olorgesailie and Mount Longonot, about thirty-five miles northwest of Nairobi, had sprayed showers of volcanic ash over the area and thus preserved the remains in layers of ash now turned into rock. It was possible that Acheulean man had cut up the carcass of an extinct elephant with some of these tools. This species of elephant, given the name *Elephus recki,* after Reck who discovered it, carried tusks eleven feet in length. A foreleg of this creature lay mixed with bolas, cleavers, and rocks, perhaps once hurled at the giant beast by prehistoric hunters.

There were also fossil evidences of a large baboon that had apparently been killed and eaten there. A picture of this extinct animal can be seen today in a showcase in the field museum at Olorgesailie. The area has become a national park thanks to Dr. Leakey and the Masai to whom the land belonged. From an elevated catwalk the visitor can see the terrain where early man made his weapons, hunted, lived and died. But in 1942, when Mary and Louis Leakey wandered into this desolate spot, there was nothing but the twisted rock, the wind and sun, and the mysterious relics of a perhaps humanlike creature.

All anthropological research was suspended during World War II. As an English Crown Colony, Kenya was an ally of Great Britain against Germany. Leakey enlisted as an army officer in charge of British Intelligence, and as part of his duties guided Allied agents through Kenya's bleak northern frontier. In addition to his position as curator of Coryndom (now called National) Museum in Nairobi, he also became a handwriting expert and amateur private detective. His military assignments were a far cry from his prewar fossil research.

While her husband engaged in war work, Mary Leakey continued exploration alone at this deserted site. Once, with their infant son, Jonathan, she took off for a lonely month's digging at Olorgesailie.

The former geology student studied the layers of rock in order to sort out the relationship between the different formations. If they later were to find fossils there, her work would help to determine their dates as well.

With the end of the war, Louis left the Criminal Investigation Department and devoted a full stint as curator of Coryndom Museum. With his family, which now included Richard, he lived in a house that was part of the museum.

With his boundless energy he started full-time excavations again. In 1946, those scientists who had refused to accept Robert Broom's ape-man were forced to change their minds. Broom inundated them with evidence to support his claims. At Sterkfontein he unearthed the crushed skull of an adolescent with six perfectly preserved teeth and a baby's skull with several milk molars. He pried loose from another stone matrix of the same period a female skull with a heavy jaw. The bones clearly belonged to an early form, which was human enough to establish the species as a possible stage between prehistoric apes and man.

After these substantial finds the opposition began to dwindle. The idea that earliest man might have come from Africa began to be generally accepted. Finally, the ruling elite of science decided to honor Broom's work. In 1947, the Royal Society of South Africa held a major gathering to celebrate the publication of a Robert Broom commemorative volume of essays. One of the most interesting and appreciated articles in it was written by his old friend and colleague, Louis S. B. Leakey. In a way the firm conviction of both men was vindicated at that meeting.

In that same year Leakey organized the first Pan African Congress of Prehistory and Quarternary Studies and prepared to return to his own excavations. With his wife he made a trip to Rusinga, on Lake Victoria, in the northeast corner, where ten years before he had found the fossil remains of an ape jaw. But on October 2, 1948, it was Mary Leakey, a respected anthropologist in her own right, who made the important discovery. Digging in the Rusinga erosion scarps, she found the tooth of an early primate, named *Proconsul* after a popular chimp in the London zoo noted for his sharp canine teeth. The skull also had prominent canine teeth. After studying the fossil, the Leakeys thought that the creature might have been a common ancestor of both ape and man. Mary flew to England to display her valuable find. The small package under her arm was insured for several thousand pounds.

In 1951, while Mary Leakey took care of a new arrival, Philip, Louis had his turn. Exploring in Kenya he dug up a few teeth of an animal then called *Sivapithecus africanus,* named for Siva, an Indian god. It was proposed that this form might be placed at the point just before man's divergence from his primate stem. While too little was known about this stage, Leakey predicted that the time would come when *Sivapithecus* might qualify as the human step that went beyond the great ape.

The combined weight of all this evidence turned world attention on Africa. Wilfrid le Gros Clark, an internationally recognized anatomist, wrote the first realistic report of African Australopithecines, the form discovered by Dart and Broom. Clark was ready to make a firm case that these early South African apes were more human than pongid (ape). Thus this hominid could be an ancestral forerunner of *Homo sapiens.*

Unfortunately, Leakey could not take immediate advantage of this change in scientific opinion. In 1952 he had to suspend his research to deal with the Mau Mau terror in Kenya. The anticolonist movement that had begun at the turn of the century had greatly escalated. As Great Britain opened more territory in East Africa to Europeans at the expense of the black Africans, resentment and anger grew. In 1952 the confrontation came to a head under the leadership of Jomo Kenyatta. The Kikuyus, tired of being exploited and oppressed, went on a rampage of violence and murder. Leakey had to carry on his duties at the Coryndom Museum with a revolver in his pocket and a policeman at his side. He was caught in a conflict between his lifelong Kikiyu friends and the British government. He acted as interpreter, negotiator, and often defender of the tribal demands. With the end of the Mau Mau uprising, he was called to the court and given the task of acting as interpreter in the trial of Kenyatta.

The nationalist leader was given nine years in a Kenyan jail.

The times were not fruitful for research either. Taking a few weeks off when he could, Leakey revisited Olduvai in the hope of finding evidence of the early men whose tools he had found in 1931. He and Mary selected forty likely sites for future exploration and then narrowed the choices down to fourteen areas in the ancient beds. But on the short, frequently interrupted expeditions they were unable to find anything. It would be another seven years before the Leakeys wrote another startling chapter in the deepening history of the human race.

The Nutcracker Man of Olduvai Gorge

On a late July afternoon in 1959, Louis and Mary Leakey sat at a wooden table perched high above Olduvai Gorge. Hanging from the roof of the open three-sided shelter, a gasoline lamp shone on the fossil bones of an extinct elephant. The two of them were waiting for dinner to be served. There would be no wild game served for the Leakeys didn't like to have the local animals hunted. They had helped to establish a national park system to protect the animals and to preserve the dwindling herds.

After supper the Leakeys went outside to watch the magnificent African sunset. The rolling hills that rimmed the canyon slowly faded from green to deep purple as the sun sank from the sky. Below them the gorge withdrew into shadow, the last rays throwing grotesque shadows across the rocky floor. Shudders in the earth had once rocked and lifted the Serengeti plains, thus enabling a mile-wide crevice to be brutally carved out. Driving rains had cut a channel through the sediments and beaten, age after age, against the stubborn stone. The Leakeys knew every mile of that barren land, had tramped innumerable times across its sun-baked floor. But they always felt, at this quiet moment of evening, the magic of the gorge, which opened up the ancient rocks that for so many thousands of years had held the secrets of man's past. They knew that down there, somewhere, was more evidence of human evolution. They might never find it, but they hoped that someday someone would.

The African night fell like a violent hand over the landscape, and the last light of the sun went out like a snuffed candle. Slowly, hesitantly, the sounds in the darkness began. Predatory beasts slipped silently away. The night creatures started their timid activity. A hyena laughed in the distance. The birds rustled and nestled in the trees overhead. Quietly, with no need to talk, the two explorers turned back to their camp. It was the end of another day. Tomorrow they would continue to work on the Frida Leakey Korongo.

The next morning Mary Leakey awoke with the first gray light of dawn. After a brisk wash in the ice-cold water, she prepared a cup of tea. When her husband appeared for breakfast, she turned toward him with a worried expression.

"You don't look well," she told him, going to get the thermometer. Louis submitted meekly and when she had checked it she frowned. "You have a temperature," she said. "You'd better not go out today."

Leakey looked gloomily at the walking stick leaning against the wall. He knew she was right. No matter how much he wanted to continue the exploration it would be unwise to take a chance on getting sick. He had become increasingly aware of the passage of time. There was never enough for what he wanted to do. It would be better to lose a day and be well enough to go out tomorrow. Disappointed, he watched Mary put on her floppy straw hat and call the two Dalmation dogs. Fortunately it was a beautiful day, with no threat of rain or a blinding dust storm. The dogs, Toots and Sally, eager to be gone, would alert her to any animals hiding in the bush. Louis waved as she disappeared down the trail into the gorge.

The morning passed quickly as he tended to a number of tasks. He looked after the minor medical needs of some Masai tribesmen who lived nearby, and then went out to feed the menagerie of animals he had collected. Just before noon he was taking some freshly baked loaves of bread out of the makeshift oven when he heard hurried footsteps on the path. To his great surprise Mary came rushing into camp.

"I've found it," she shouted breathlessly. "It's the lead to man, our man. Come quickly!"

Leakey jammed a hat on his head and ran outside. Together they climbed into their jeep and raced down the steep, twisting road to the excavation site. When they arrived at the Frida Leakey Korongo, Mary pointed and Leakey rattled to a stop. The spot was marked with a cairn of low stones. Leakey jumped out of the car and knelt on the parched earth. Immediately he saw a fossilized human temporal bone that was lodged in a rock slide. Farther up the slope were two immense premolar teeth, powerful enough to crack nuts. Hence, the name Nutcracker man.

"Dear boy," Leakey said, and knelt in prayer, "we've waited a long time for you." They had finally found the remains of a hominid (manlike animal) who had inhabited the rocky expanse of Olduvai Gorge.

After the initial excitement of the spectacular find, the hard, painstaking work began. The Leakeys had to free what proved to be four hundred pieces of a human skull from the grip of the resistant rock. With a camel's hairbrush and dental picks they spent almost three weeks disinterring the pieces from the solid matrix. With tireless

13
Mystery Murder of a Prehistoric Child

It was in the early part of 1960 that Dr. Leakey worked with his son Jonathan at a prehistoric site a few hundred yards north of the spot where Nutcracker man had been found. Ever since his parents had introduced him to the mystery and beauty of Olduvai's strange world, Jonathan had been fascinated with this wild area he knew as well as the streets of Nairobi. When the eighteen-year-old youth discovered the jawbone of a saber-toothed tiger, his father was extremely proud of him. It was the first such fossil ever unearthed in East Africa. Louis encouraged him to keep searching in the same place for traces of the man who might once have hunted the fierce animal. A search party joined him to sift through the soil to find a specimen that would add another date to the human calendar.

On a blisteringly hot morning a few weeks later, Jonathan saw something gleam in the fossil bed at his feet. Wild with excitement he called a staff assistant. "Look what I've found," he cried. "It's a human jaw!"

The African worker took one look and shouted to the rest of the crew, "Johnny's got it! Come quickly."

The young man hurriedly radioed his father at his suburban home in Nairobi. Leakey couldn't get back fast

patience the digging crew removed and sifted tons of scree (pebbles) from beneath the rock in an effort to save every delicate fragment of the priceless discovery. Finally, after more time-consuming work, they had pieced together the clue to a complex crossword puzzle, the lower part of the skull. It appeared to be the skull of an eighteen-year-old youth.

Leakey gave him the official name of *Zinjanthropus boisei*. *Zinj* comes from the old Arabic word for East Africa, and *anthropus* from the Greek word for man, and *boisei* from Boise, a British financial backer. To get an estimate of the correct age of this being dug out of the potassium-bearing rock, Louis sent a sample of the hardened volcanic ash from the site at Olduvai to the University of California at Berkeley. The earth science department of that famous university sent back a most startling answer on the date of Zinj. Through the potassium argon method, a reliable way of dating volcanic ash, geologists revealed that *Zinjanthropus,* a manlike creature, roamed the plains 1,750,000 years ago.

In trying to reconstruct what the being looked like, Dr. Leakey imagined a creature slightly shorter than a gorilla, who walked erect on two feet. With a flat forehead, high cheekbones and heavy eye ridges, he had the appearance of an ape. But his heavily worn molars showed a kinship with the Australopithecines of South Africa, regarded as more than an ape if not quite a man. There was evidence that *Zinjanthropus* may have had enough intelligence to make tools as on the same site there were definite artifacts of lava and chert. Also scattered in the area was raw material suitable for the manufacture of chopping tools.

Leakey proposed a picture of a hominid who lived by eating vegetables and nuts, as well as birds, rodents, snakes, and lizards. For a change of diet he may have cracked the shells of turtles and caught catfish in small pools. To attack small game he probably used a club or some other portable weapon. It seemed clear, however, that he wasn't a great hunter. He didn't have the implements to attack larger animals. If he were lucky he might come upon a massive *Dinotherium* trapped in a bog or wounded in a battle. With his light, sharp-edged pieces of stone he could have hacked away chunks of meat.

The skull of the creature that Leakey called *Zinjanthropus* triggered much controversy and confusion among prehistorians. *Zinjanthropus* seemed to be rather old to have been a toolmaker, but he was found in association with a large number of chipped stone tools. The question was made all the more tantalizing when further investigation revealed that *Zinjanthropus* was actually the same as *Paranthropus,* or *Australopithecus robustus* as many anthropologists refer to the Leakey find today.

If *Zinjanthropus* did not make the tools found around his bones, then who did? John T. Robinson, an assistant to Broom, proposed that the tools were made by a gracile Australopithecine whose bones were also found in Olduvai. Later finds tended to uphold this view, and Leakey modified his opinions accordingly.

The relationship between *Zinjanthropus (Paranthropus)* and the gracile *Australopithecus* is still not fully resolved. A prevailing opinion is that *Paranthropus* represents a "dead end" in human evolution while *Australopithecus africanus,* the gracile form, may have been in the direct line of that evolution. *Paranthropus* eventually became extinct, possibly losing out in competition with the more advanced Australopithocines. The fossil evidence does seem to indicate that *Paranthropus* and *Australopithecus* types lived at the same time in the same place.

Soon after he found *Zinjanthropus,* Leakey fessor Richard L. Hay, a geologist from E spend the summer at Olduvai Gorge. Hay call a geologist's paradise. After exploring the a supported Leakey's claim that man's evolu much farther back than the commonly accep years, that it indeed had started over three number of years ago. He even went so far as t Java man and Peking man as the oldest ho asserted that *Zinjanthropus* had roamed the g Africa a million years before these other form in Asia. When he returned to Berkeley he took stone tool Leakey had given him. Sitting in h studied the primitive implement and observed hills above this building men are drilling into t the atoms with streams of accelerated particl tory to space travel. And to think that it bega chopper from the time of Zinj."

enough, and when he arrived he helped chip out of the matrix the rest of the find, the hand bones, teeth, and skull of a child, and the nearly complete set of an adult's foot bones. Then he set to work using his knowledge as an anatomist. Spreading the bones on the table in front of him, he pointed to the jaw. "This fossil belonged to a child about ten or twelve years old," he observed. "The teeth tell this. The first molars are worn down with use. The second molars show little decay. There is no sign of the third molar, which comes around the age of sixteen."

"But how about the bones of the child's hand?" Jonathan asked him.

Leakey studied the skeletal remains. "It doesn't look like a modern hand," he said. "But I believe that this child had some ability to grasp small objects." He looked uneasily at another fossil. "But there is something alarming about this child's skull."

Picking up the object he pointed to a hair-line fracture. "I don't think that this child died from disease. It looks as though death came from a blow on the skull."

Jonathan suggested that perhaps the child had fallen and hit his head on a rock. Leakey disagreed. He was convinced that the blow came from a blunt instrument. He commented sadly that this might well be an example of one of man's first crimes against his own kind. Then he turned his attention to the other specimens.

He indicated the bones of the adult foot Jonathan had found. "This bone is nearer to that of a human being than of the other primates. You can see how the big toe is closer to the second one. Lacking is the wide separation you would find in the toes of apes and monkeys." He speculated on a further fossil, the most exciting discovered at the Child Site. "This adult collar bone resembles human collarbones. This raises the possibility that the

111

child and adult were closer to being forerunners of man than was *Zinjanthropus.*"

But was it a true man? The line between ancient apes and man, as it was pushed farther backward, became thinner and thinner. Potassium argon tests estimated the fossils found at the Child Site at almost two million years. It appeared that a hominid had existed even before *Zinjanthropus.* But Leakey had too many doubts to definitely classify the child and adult of the pre-Zinj period as a type of human. As a result he was not prepared to give the fossils a scientific name. Nevertheless, he did believe that with further research this creature might well turn out to be an early hominid.

These remains had raised the question of who made the tools in Bed I. Leakey wrote, in *Unveiling Man's Origin,* "that in view of this new discovery it was no longer justifiable to assume," as he had earlier, "that *Zinjanthropus* made the tools found with him. Instead, three alternatives now had to be faced: a) that the new hominid, who was more like today's man, was the toolmaker, not *Zinjanthropus;* or b) that *Zinjanthropus* was the toolmaker notwithstanding the presence of another contemporary hominid; or c) that both might have made the primitive tools that were found in Bed I."

Meanwhile, in December of 1960, the Leakey family made another momentous find. Louis and his youngest son, Philip, had climbed to the top of a hill above Bed II. It was pure chance that had earlier led him to find this "living floor" strewn with animal bones and tools of the lower Acheulean culture. That same good fortune would lead them to another discovery that day. As they scrambled down the face of the cliff they pushed back the heavy branches in their way. Reaching up to clear some brush, Louis stopped in his tracks. He stepped closer and then dropped to his knees. A bone was protruding from the undergrowth. He stared a moment at the human skull and then leaped to his feet and called Mary, who was working nearby. He had found the creature who used the weapons and killed the animals found in Bed II.

He afterward commented that it was lucky that the light had been just right that day. "I might not have found this site for months," he added. "By that time erosion might have destroyed the skull forever." From his college days he had been well aware that luck had played a great part in his discoveries. But in response to those who called his family the "Lucky Leakeys," he pointed out that "for thirty years I've been digging without ever giving up."

Lucky or not, another member of the family also made his contribution to our knowledge of the world in which early man had lived. Richard Leakey, the sixteen-year-old second son, found the fossil bones of *Dinotherium*. Expertly using a dental pick and paint brush, the young explorer carefully removed the fossil elephant from its hard bed. Nearby on the canyon floor were shortly later dug up, the bones of the giant pig, an antlered giraffe, and a mammoth sheep. Richard patiently went to work on them as well. The value of his discovery was confirmed by his father when Louis said, "We can't tell for certain, but there is a high probability that Chellean (lower Acheulean) man was a stem from which modern man developed."

While Jonathan remained at Olduvai in charge of provisions, vehicle repair, and operation of the radio, Louis shifted operations to the orange groves of a Kenyan farmer at Fort Ternan. Fred Wicker had sent Leakey some intriguing specimens from a rock outcrop that was located on his farm. Leaving his competent family to explore Olduvai, Louis was off on another adventure.

14

Was Homo habilis the Parent of the Astronauts?

It was midway in the season as Dr. Leakey was rallying a digging team at Fort Ternan for the onslaught on the face of the rock outcrop when he was urgently called to another fossil front. He was intensively pursuing a search for a clue to the human ancestor wherever he could find it. Fortunately he was leaving in charge of the excavation Heselon Mukiri, a dedicated Kikuyu staff member with whom he had worked closely over many years.

On a perfect afternoon in July, Heselon Mukiri hammered away at the rock face at Fort Ternan, his eyes intently studying the stone under each blow of his pick. Suddenly he saw something. He rapidly chipped away at it until enough of the bone fossils were exposed to confirm what he had already guessed. The fragments of upper jaw and lower molar looked different from anything he had seen before. They did not appear to belong to an ape.

He radioed Leakey immediately. When the anthropologist arrived at the Wicker farm site he was jubilant. Mukiri had found what proved to be a major breakthrough in the unraveling of prehistory. Later data by potassium argon testing of the fossils showed that the owner of the jaw had existed some 14 million years ago. Leakey was not quite sure of what he had found. "This fossil primate was not a man," he wrote. "Neither was he an ape. The unique creature would seem to be heading toward man without really being one." He gave the subhuman the name *Kenyapithecus wickeri* in honor of the perceptive farmer and the country where he lived.

Later he offered a more detailed explanation *Kenyapithecus wickeri* in *National Geographic* magazine. "This jaw belongs to a primate who is near to man. He had a very small canine tooth and thus not as long as those found in animals. The lower molar has a crown more like that of man than ape. This prehuman creature had one essential trait of present-day man, one never found in the same form among fossil or living apes. It is what scientists call 'canine fossa.' This in humans is a depression in the upper jaw that anchors a muscle to control lip movements of speech. But the 'canine fossa' did not give the fossil primate the ability to speak."

Accordingly, Leakey did not go so far as to claim that *Kenyapithecus wickeri* belonged to the hominid family. In his view it was more likely that this early creature represented a stage leading to both man and ape. He concluded that while true apes could be accurately traced far back in time, this was not true for forms of early man. More likely, in some far past era, a protohominid had started on a different evolutionary path from the proto apes of the same era. *Proto,* of course, means "first in time."

There was no denying the elation in his tone when he summed it up: "Until the discovery of *Kenyapithecus* we had generally no information about any stage of man in that vast stretch of time since the *Proconsul* family of Miocene apes. *Kenyapithecus* filled an enormous gap in the panorama of man's development between the time of *Proconsul* who lived 25 million years ago and *Zinjanthropus* of Olduvai at 1,750,000 years."

At Fort Ternan there was an added bonus among the fossils. At the time of *Kenyapithecus wickeri* there were violent geologic upheavals in the area. Apparently at one point subterranean shifts caused enormous volcanic activity, and thousands of animals were trapped in the deadly rain of lava ash. The substance that killed them also preserved their bones, and by cutting through the stone layers Leakey was given a view into the far past. A bantam rhino left his jaw, and an elephant fossil added more evidence to the effect that in the early period of development the beast was the size of a small horse. Another diminutive creature, the extinct giraffe, was only as large as a donkey. Leakey noted that many of the fossil bones were smashed. He felt that *Kenyapithecus wickeri* might have used stones to break up animal skulls for brains and marrow.

As Dr. Leakey told a group of newsmen in Washington, D.C., "These prehumans had started to make use of animal food to add to their vegetable diet. Not having a large canine tooth, *Kenyapithecus* might have been forced to put his hands into action. Making a hammer with a stone, this subhuman creature might have broken up some animal bones. Too, the crude stone hammer came in handy to crack nuts when food was scarce."

Leakey drove back and forth from Fort Ternan to Olduvai Gorge. There in 1962, workers dug up the human jaw of a young woman apparently caught unexpectedly in a volcanic eruption 800,000 years ago. Nicknamed Cinderella, her remains were classified as belonging to the same group of hominids found at the Child Site. The major difference was that the young child had met its violent death a million years earlier. Leakey called it *Homo habilis,* from the Latin meaning, "man having ability." He could not be more specific than that.

Later he stated to the National Press Club in Washington, "*Homo habilis* may rank some day as the most important in our knowledge of human evolution. This type of man is unquestionably shattering to our whole concept of man. Evidence from this find might have rewritten the story of early man. This 'man of ability' could well have stayed around to become the father of modern man." He confidently added, "There is no doubt that Africa is where man really comes from. Darwin's theory of evolution is no longer a theory. It's a fact."

As Dr. Leakey sketched the development of this early hominid over millions of years, it became clear what the species had had to do simply to survive. *Homo habilis* possessed a larger braincase than the doomed *Zinjanthropus.* Only three feet high, he may have been too small to secure food or defend himself by brute strength alone. He had to use his brain.

Slowly, over tens of thousands of years, he learned to utilize the natural objects he found scattered about him. Through trial and error, he became clever with his hands and began to shape crude stone tools that improved his chances to live. Starting with the sharp edge of a rock, accidentally found, he later developed a stone knife patiently chipped to an efficient edge or point. The wonder of this step—no other animal is capable of it—is the impulse behind the effort. That first impulse, even in its most primitive form, is the same as the technical skill that created the computer and sent men hundreds of thousands of miles to explore the surface of the moon. Without *Homo habilis,* sophisticated space exploration would have been impossible.

With a third major discovery in 1963, the outlines of an arresting theory began to take form. Again a member of Louis's crew, Heselon Mukiri, found a human fossil washed onto the surface in Maiko Gulley at Olduvai. It was in fragments because Masai cattle coming down to drink had trampled the skull. But after piecing it together and carefully studying "Poor George" (named by Mary Leakey), Leakey concluded that the species was a true hominid and not an earlier near-man. This African fossil closely resembled the earlier *Pithecanthropus (Homo erectus)* of China and Java.

Leakey now believed he had dramatic proof that there were three separate lines, all existing at about the same time, which had haltingly evolved toward human status in the ancient plains. One was an example of *Homo erectus;* a second was *Homo habilis* moving toward *Homo sapiens;* the third was *Zinjanthropus (Paranthropus)* heading toward extinction. At first most scientists thought Louis had finally gone too far. His reputation for fantastic claims was well known. But these same men had to grudgingly admit that each time, however absurd his theories might have seemed, many scientists believed them to be quite plausible.

In recognition of their tireless exploration and outstanding prehistoric research, the National Geographic Society awarded its Hubbard Medal to Mary and Louis Leakey. The famous couple flew to Washington where Chief Justice Earl Warren made the presentation in Constitution Hall. Leakey thanked the society for its continued support over the years. Then he made a statement which was as meaningful to him as any of his discoveries. He said, "This medal belongs not to two Leakeys, but to five. Whatever we have done, we have done together."

15
The Protohominids

In the 1960s as director of the Center for Prehistory and Paleontology, in Nairobi, Dr. Leakey publicly displayed fragments of seven beings he claimed belonged to yet another new species. In the middle 1960s, on the basis of fossil remains from Rusinga Island and the Songhor beds in Northern Kenya, he claimed identification of another hominid. He named this Miocene creature *Kenyapithecus africanus*. Many authorities think it a *Ramapithecus*. The pygmy-sized hominid, with its chin slightly protruding in front of its teeth, lived at the same time as *Proconsul,* but at some earlier stage its ancestors had developed along different lines. As Leakey commented, "This find predates many of man's forbears previously unearthed by at least six million years. It is now possible to see the family from which we evolved twenty million years ago by *Kenyapithecus africanus.*"

While most of his scientific colleagues supported his view, he quickly qualified it by adding that the manlike creature was not a toolmaker. Early hominids didn't learn to use tools until perhaps 12 million years ago. This was all the more puzzling because the chimpanzee is quite adept at utilizing simple tools such as sticks. This ape can insert a stick into a termite hill and lick the insects clinging to his hand-held implement like a child with a Popsicle.

Another hominid that played a vital role in the development of man wasn't a toolmaker either. *Ramapithecus brevirostris* was first dug up by G. Edward Lewis in the Siwalik Hills of India in 1936. But there were challengers to the Yale geologist's claim that this fossil primate was a hominid. They insisted that the Asian skeleton looked more like an ape than a man. Thus *Ramapithecus* gathered dust on a remote museum shelf. It wasn't until 1964 that a Yale anthropologist found fragments of the jaw and teeth of the same creature in India. With this added evidence, Professor Elwyn Simon was able to prove that the animal was a recognizable hominid. More important, *Ramapithecus brevirostris* was dated as living 12 million years ago, in the same Upper Miocene period as *Kenyapithecus wickeri*. It was clear to Leakey that these two creatures could have been successively possible ancestors of modern man. In fact, *Ramapithecus* and *Kenyapithecus* may be the same species.

However, as usual, other scientists violently disagreed. In 1967 university scholars at Berkeley set the final separation of pongid (ape) and hominid (man or his direct ancestors) at the much later (more recent) date of 5 million years. Allan Wilson and Vincent Sarich based their findings on a new method of dating, "the protein clock," which Leakey was greatly opposed to. This unusual technique, a complete departure from the methods paleontologists had always used, depended on a dated map of molecules. The molecular biologists concentrated on the makeup of proteins, especially albumin—the substance found in blood serum—and hemoglobin, the red coloring matter in blood corpuscles. They found that the protein in these two substances evolved, over a great span of years, at a constant rate. Since the animals in question have a common ancestor, these scientists could "read" the protein content and thus suggest the length of time the animals under debate have been following separate evolutionary paths.

In one analysis, they compared the blood protein of a number of different living animal species. They found that human albumin closely resembles the albumin in the blood of Rhesus (Indian) monkeys. Further, they discovered that the albumin of man, chimpanzee, and gorilla are only one-sixth as different from each other as they are from the albumin of the Rhesus. This meant that man and pongid (ape) diverged from a common evolutionary tree six times more recently than did man and the Rhesus monkey. Since they assumed that the time of divergence between man and monkey can't be greater than 30 million years ago, Wilson and Sarich calculated that man and the apes separated about 5 million years ago. In addition to this albumin evidence, the scientists found that the other protein, hemoglobin, is exactly the same in man and chimpanzee. That makes them close biological relatives, for instance as close as the sheep and the goat. By the same test, man is related to the ape as closely as the horse is to the donkey. Although this supported Leakey's contention that man and primate apes were related, it considerably shortened the age between modern man and the first human ancestor.

Leakey refused to accept the conclusions of the protein clock technique. Elwyn Simons agreed with him, for both men continued to believe that man and ape branched off far earlier than 5 million years ago. For proof they offered the protohominid fossils—*Kenyapithecus africanus* and *Ramapithecus brevirostris*. But the two University of California biologists countered this. Sarich insisted that if

Ramapithecus was indeed 14 million years old (like *Kenyapithecus* whom it resembled), it couldn't be labeled a hominid. He was equally insistent about the bones of *Kenyapithecus.* Sarich accepted the age of the fossils, between 20 and 22 million years, but he wouldn't recognize them as manlike. He preferred to consider them as belonging to an early chimpanzee that lived far too early to be a human ancestor. It was to become a conflict not just between two interpretations, but between two generations of prehistorians. Leakey would not accept the new methods. Sarich and Wilson would not accept the old.

Unlike the younger men, this was nothing new to Louis Leakey. He had faced such opposition many times before. His resistance was not due to the fact that his methods had become old-fashioned and he was unable to change. He had always been willing to re-examine his theories in the light of new evidence to change them.

He had once had a book already at the printers and recalled it when he radically changed his point of view on the subject. But this time he felt that he was right in considering *Kenyapithecus africanus* a protohominid who lived 20 million years ago.

The origins of man are still shrouded in doubt. The common ancestor of ape and man, the creature that separated from that ancestor to become modern *Homo sapiens,* the dates when this evolution occurred, the length of time it took, have yet to be resolved. If Leakey's theory is true, then the only true protohominids are *Kenyapithecus* and *Ramapithecus.* Yet even this leaves us with some questions. As Leakey himself asks in *Unveiling Man's Origin,* did a separate branch of the family of hominids to which *Ramapithecus* belongs evolve in the Far East into *Homo erectus,* Peking and Java man? Or did *Ramapithe-*

cus slowly move from Africa to the Far East and then develop there? Or, conversely, did he migrate from Java and China to Africa, and evolve independently there? The answers are still to be discovered.

The other major conflict that remains to be explored is which line of ascent is the real one. Many scientists believe that *Homo erectus,* as seen in Peking and Java man, is our direct ancestor. Leakey believed, and other noted scholars concur, that modern *Homo sapiens* comes from the species of *Homo habilis.* Recent evidence tends to support this latter view, but the proof is far from conclusive, and much work needs to be done.

The case for *Homo habilis* was strengthened in the late 1960s when an even older specimen was discovered by an International Expedition to Africa. Through Leakey's efforts, Emperor Haile Selassie gave permission for exploration in the Omo Valley in southeast Ethiopia. Three teams, from the United States, France, and Kenya, joined forces to excavate the site. Unable to participate himself, Leakey invited his twenty-two-year-old son, Richard, to lead the Kenya group.

In 1967, the international scientists under the leadership of F. Clark Howell, then from the University of Chicago, went into the Omo Valley and found one of the most startling fossils ever unearthed. It was a close call, because the American team almost threw it away. They thought the jaw with fifty teeth belonged to a hog. As it turned out, the fossil may be the oldest human ancestor ever discovered. It was closely related to the *Homo habilis* of the Olduvai Gorge. As Louis Leakey told an American television audience, the Omo fossil dated back almost 4 million years and provided more evidence that Africa is the cradle of man. Haile Selassie of Ethiopia was so impressed with the find that he awarded Leakey the Gold Medal and a prize for African research valued at over ten thousand dollars.

The next few years were to be filled with prizes and honors, which inevitably found their way to a little used drawer or forgotten shelf in the Leakey home. The most valuable gift the famous scientist could have received was more time. There was never enough. On many occasions he prayed for a seventy-two hour day. There were lectures in Israel, India, and the United States. There were expeditions to plan, findings to study, professional meetings to attend. The "universal man," as he has been called—anthropologist, anatomist, zoologist, and archeologist—was in demand for consultation all over the world.

While he was away, the family continued to explore for prehistoric remains in East Africa. Dr. Mary Leakey found yet another *Homo habilis* at Olduvai in 1969. Jonathan Leakey, who works part time as a fossil hunter, follows a dangerous career on the shore of Lake Baringo in northern Kenya. On his reptile farm he handles some of Africa's deadliest snakes to extract venom for medical laboratories. Philip became a student in geology at the Duke of York School in Nairobi, and could be seen in television documentaries leading climbers up the slopes of Mount Kenya.

Richard Leakey has entered the field of prehistory as a career. When he represented Kenya in the International Expedition he discovered many valuable fossils but because of his lack of academic background had to turn them over to scientists with doctoral degrees. As a result, he decided to attend the University College in Nairobi. Still torn between fieldwork and formal study, he found time to organize several expeditions with grants from the National Geographic Society. His favorite fossil territory is the desolate country in Northern Kenya around Lake Turkhana south of the Omo Valley. Like his father, he is completely at home in a black people's country. A white man who thinks like an African, he speaks Swahili fluently and is knowledgeable about the traditions and customs of the newly independent nation of Kenya.

The Leakeys were particularly proud of their second son when he showed promise of becoming a better prehistorian than they were. On an expedition in May of 1969 around Lake Turkhana, Kay Behrensmeyer, the geologist in Richard's group, found choppers and sharp-edged flakes of basalt that were set by potassium argon analysis experts at 2.6 million years old. If this date is correct, they are the earliest known stone tools. In August, Richard discovered a fossil creature even older than the *Zinjanthropus* found by his mother at Olduvai. Richard's specimen is likely to be dated at almost 3 million years.

When Mary Leakey flew up from Olduvai Gorge, Richard told her how he had stumbled on the fossil by sheer luck. He was walking along a dry bed and happened to glance at a thorn bush he was about to pass. Had he been walking faster he might have missed it. Lying behind the bush was the nearly complete skull of an early hominid. A bony ridge above the eye sockets of the skull clearly indicated it as an *Australopithecine*. Mary Leakey called the fossil "beautiful and absolutely magnificent."

When Louis arrived on the scene, five hundred miles from Nairobi, he marveled at the fossil's marked resemblance to Nutcracker man. He was especially impressed that his son's find belonged to a hominid that had lived hundreds of thousands of years before *Zinjanthropus* as well as hundreds of miles away. But he refused to attribute the discovery to chance. What gratified him most was that he had been able to pass on the teachings of his

Kikuyu elders to his son. As he was later to write, any success he had had as a fossil hunter was due to his early training as a Kikuyu youth. That rigorous education taught him "two things, patience—especially patience—and observation. In some parts of Africa, survival depends upon your reaction to irregularities in your surroundings. A torn leaf, a paw print, a bush that rustles when there is no breeze, a sudden quiet—these are the signals that spell the difference between life and death.

"The same instant recognition of something different—a glint of white in the face of a cliff, an odd-shaped pebble, a tiny fragment of bone—leads to the discovery of fossils. And patience. I can still hear the Kikuyu elders telling the boys of my age over and over, 'Be patient, be careful, don't hurry. Try again and again and again.'"

16
The Last Years

In 1970 Louis Leakey arrived in London for the first lap of a lecture tour that would help him raise $300,000 for yearly research. But before he could change planes for New York he suffered a serious heart attack. At first he wasn't worried because he had already suffered two previous attacks, in 1967 and 1968, and had fully recovered from them after brief stays in the hospital. What he didn't know was that this time it would be different. After spending a few weeks in a London hospital he gained enough strength to fly back to his home in Langata, a suburb of Nairobi, for an extended rest. For an incredibly energetic man who worked long hours every day of the year such a period could be unbearably frustrating.

In many ways it proved otherwise. Louis was now able to spend time in his garden working with his roses and carnations, and tending the orchids planted by his youngest son, Philip. It was also a chance to see more of his family. Mary, Richard, and Philip were at home, Colin was nearby teaching at the University of Makerere in Kampala, Uganda, and Jonathan frequently drove down from northern Kenya. His only daughter, Priscilla, was living in England. The enforced vacation gave him the time to catch up on his reading. He was gratified to see books and articles by young prehistorians who had been inspired by his own work. Far more important to him than the honors he had won was the fact that he had encouraged a new generation of scientists to enter an often frustrating, though sometimes rewarding, field of study.

The work of one of these young people particularly interested him. Under his urging, Jane van Lawick-Goodall had conducted an unprecedented experiment. She had lived on and off for ten years in the wilds of Tanzania with a tribe of chimpanzees. No one had ever recorded the behavior of any animal in such detail before. Her findings proved invaluable for the study of man. In her book, *In the Shadow of Man,* Goodall draws important parallels between early human and modern chimpanzee behavior. She found that the chimpanzee could use a branch or stick for a weapon and that, contrary to opinion, he was not exclusively a vegetarian. He occasionally killed and ate many other animals. Also, he was far more dexterous than had been imagined, using stones to break open nuts and manipulating sticks to dislodge termites and other hidden insects.

As a result of his protégé's work, Leakey wrote in *Adam or Ape* that he had revised his former definition of man. Previously he had declared that man emerged at that point in primate evolution when tools were used consistently in a regular pattern. He changed this to a more specific statement: man was the primate who first shaped and employed cutting tools. Citing Goodall's firsthand observation, he was able to strengthen his argument that man's earliest ancestors can be better understood by studying present-day primates. Typically, Louis Leakey, once stubborn, the teacher and renowned prehistorian, was learning from his younger colleagues and, with more flexibility, was revising his own theories in the light of their further evidence.

It was impossible for Leakey to remain inactive, and after months of rest he returned to the lecture circuit. As always, there was the pressing need for money, this time for the Leakey Foundation established in Los Angeles for prehistoric research. Thus Louis arrived in San Francisco in May of 1971 to participate in a televised symposium. But misfortune was to continue to plague him. He fell from the podium at the Public Broadcasting System studio and for a moment it was feared that he had suffered another heart attack. Everyone knew that he was not sufficiently recovered to maintain the rigorous schedule he had set himself. But after a short rest in a local hospital—it proved not to have been a heart attack after all—he continued his activities. He insisted on keeping a date to lecture at the University of California at Berkeley. When he appeared on the stage of Zellerbach Hall with his walking stick the packed house gave him an ovation. He proceeded to launch into his subject with all the vigor of a young man.

It was to be a spirited discussion. Dr. Sherwood Washburn, a distinguished anthropologist, was seated in the audience and he confronted Leakey with the Wilson-Sarich criticisms. Leakey, in his turn, spiritedly defended his position. He rejected protein analysis and with the aid of carefully prepared charts proceeded to demolish the technique point by point. Finally, Washburn was forced to admit that though he still disagreed with the eminent scientist he did respect his view. He went on to praise Leakey for his considerable contributions; whatever their differences there was no doubt that Leakey had pushed the frontiers of prehistoric research far into man's past.

The following October the white African addressed another audience, this time in Washington, D.C. It was a familiar theme. He was as confident as ever that new discoveries would revolutionize man's thinking about himself, and that the younger scientists would do this work in the near future. He dwelt at some length on the specific areas that needed to be explored, and encouraged his colleagues to devote themselves to this all-important research. He continued his plea for more funds to open up valuable sites where evidence of early man could be found.

One such site was in the Suguta in the desolate Northern Frontier, an area so difficult of access that it could only be reached by a four-wheeled jeep. A digging crew would have to endure a three-day trip over bone-rattling roads into the rocky desert occasionally swept by hurricane winds. It was not an expedition that many men would have considered, let alone encouraged. But three years before Leakey had been impressed with the possibilities of the site. He had dispatched his son Philip to look over the area. That was all Leakey needed. With his characteristic enthusiasm he set out to explore it.

In August of 1972 Richard Leakey made another startling discovery on the eastern bank of Lake Rudolf (Lake Turkhana). He led an expedition that unearthed a human skull splintered into hundreds of fragments. It was found buried beneath volcanic ash dated at 2.6 million years. The ancient skull was almost half again as large as that of modern man. It was also considerably larger than some specimens of skulls found in younger deposits. This meant that man's brain evolved far earlier than had been formerly believed. Also dug up at the site were limb bones quite similar to modern man. They indicated that this prehistoric being was capable of traveling long distances on two legs and in an erect posture. In layers of much the same age, the team of California anthropologist Glynn

Isaac has found stone tools and the traces of campsites and of food-sharing activities by the early protohumans.

In labeling the skull as human, Richard Leakey relied on studies made years before by his father. He had to decide where to place this new find among *Australopithecus,* a man-ape living 3.5 to 4.5 million years ago, and *Homo erectus,* a genuinely manlike creature a million years old. While some scientists believed that *Homo erectus* evolved from *Australopithecus,* Richard was as stubborn as his father in insisting that *Homo erectus* is not a true human ancestor. Instead, he affirmed that this new find is the real human parent. His claim only added to the controversy, for the skull pushed the date of man's origins even farther back in time—a million years older than *Zinjanthropus* and half a million older than *Homo habilis.* He was not surprised to have his theory met by violent disagreement. In stirring up scientific storms he was only following in the tradition of his illustrious father.

It is not often that a man lives to see his work carried on by his son, and Leakey was proud and delighted at Richard's independent discovery. It was possibly the oldest human skull ever found. He looked forward with considerable pleasure to the symposium in London where Richard would present his scientific report. But, unfortunately, he was never to enjoy this crowning event.

In late September, in the middle of his sixty-ninth year, Louis Leakey suffered a final heart attack in London. He was rushed to St. Stephen's Hospital but on Sunday, October 1, 1972, he died. He might have lengthened his life somewhat if he had listened to his doctor's orders and retired from lecturing, fund raising, and the scientific inquiry that took him around the world. But he wasn't that kind of man. If he was to live, he had to live as he always had, vigorously, enthusiastically, totally committed to his work. For him, there could be no other way.

The scientific community had lost one of its greatest men and one of its most stimulating and exciting personalities. In the course of his career he had won the highest honors—in 1953 he had been awarded the Doctor of Science degree from Oxford, in 1963 the Doctor of Laws degree from Berkeley, in 1966 he had been made an Honorary Fellow of the British Academy, and in 1969 the Doctor of Laws degree from the University of Gelph in Canada. Dr. Melvin Payne, president of the National Geographic Society, commemorated his passing with the following words: "Louis Leakey brilliantly rewrote the history of man as his astonishing fossil discoveries in Africa revolutionized our concept of man's development. Those who have known him will deeply miss this protean man." The word is apt. He was protean in his energy and in his interests, a man who found his world and its beginnings full of wonder and dedicated himself to it without regard to personal cost.

On October 4, in the country of his birth, Louis Leakey was buried alongside his parents at All Saint's Church in Limuru after a private service around the grave. A few days later, at a memorial service held in All Saint's Cathedral in Nairobi, the Honorable C. Njonjo, Kenya's Attorney-General representing Jomo Kenyatta, paid him what must remain the final compliment. "He cannot be thought of as a member of a tribe, race or country," the Honorable Njonjo said, "but as a member of the human race to enlighten the world on the possible origins of mankind. We are all a little prouder for having known him." It was a tribute that, above all others, Leakey himself would have appreciated.

Bibliography

Ardrey, Robert. *African Genesis*. New York: Atheneum, 1961.

Burkitt, Miles. *Old Stone Age*. New York: Atheneum, 1963.

Clark, Grahame. *Stone Age Hunters*. New York: McGraw-Hill, 1967.

Clarke, W. E. *Antecedents of Man:* An Introduction to the Evolution of the Primates. Chicago: Quadrangle Books, 1971.

————. *Fossil Evidence for Human Evolution:* An Introduction to the Study of Paleoanthropology. Chicago: University of Chicago Press, 1964.

Coon, Carleton. *Origin of Races*. New York: Alfred A. Knopf, Inc., 1962.

Daniel, Glyn. *The Idea of Prehistory*. New York: Penguin Books, 1972.

Dickinson, Alice. *Charles Darwin and Natural Selection*. New York: Franklin Watts, 1964.

Edey, Maitland, A. *The Missing Link*. New York: Time-Life Books, 1963.

Howell, F. Clark. *Early Man*. New York: Time-Life Books, 1973.

Howells, William. *Mankind in the Making:* The Story of Human Evolution, Rev. Ed. New York: Doubleday, 1973.

Lawick-Goodall, Jane van. *In the Shadow of Man*. Boston: Houghton Mifflin, 1971.

Leakey, Louis, S. B. *Stone Age Races of Kenya,* Second Ed. New York: Oxford University Press, 1970.

————. *Kenya: Contrasts & Problems*. Cambridge: Schenkman Pub. Co., 1966.

————. *White African:* An Early Autobiography. Cambridge: Schenkman Pub. Co., 1966.

————. *The Stone Age Cultures of Kenya Colony*. London: Frank Cass, Ltd., 1971.

————. *Adam's Ancestors:* The Evolution of Man & His Culture. New York: Harper & Row, 1953.

————, and Goodall, Vanne, M. *Unveiling Man's Origin*. Cambridge: Schenkman Pub. Co., 1969.

————, edited. *Adam or Ape:* A Sourcebook of Discoveries about Early Man. Cambridge: Schenkman Pub. Co., 1971.

————. *Olduvai Gorge Vol. I + II:* Nineteen Fifty-One—Nineteen Sixty-One. New York: Cambridge University Press, 1965.

Leet, Lewis, D. and Leet, Florence, J. eds. *World of Geology*. New York: McGraw-Hill, 1961.

Martin, Christopher. *Wonders of Prehistoric Man*. New York: Putnam, 1964.

Moore, Ruth. *Man, Time and Fossils,* Rev. Ed. New York: Alfred A. Knopf, 1961.

Oakley, Kenneth. *Man the Tool-maker,* Third Ed. Chicago: University of Chicago Press, 1960.

Perkins, Carol Morse. *Shattered Skull*. New York: Atheneum, 1965.

Pfeiffer, John E. *The Emergence of Man*. New York: Harper & Row, 1972.

von Koeningswald, G. H. *The Evolution of Man,* Rev. Ed. Ann Arbor: University of Michigan Press, 1975.

Index

Index

man, prehistoric (*Cont.*):
  age of, *see* dating, methods of
  Asia as possible birthplace of,
    57–58, 59, 68–69
  Biblical dates of origin, 24
  burial customs of, 56, 66
  diet of, 107–108, 116
  Europe as possible birthplace
    of, 57, 59
  as hunter, 19–21
  Leakey's definitions of, 128
  pottery of, 76–77, 81
  as tool user, 24, 26, 27, 59, 90,
    98–99, 117, 119, 123, 128
  *see also specific types of
    prehistoric man*
Man's Place in Nature, 49–50
Markgraf, Richard, 59
Marston, Dr. Alvan, 96
Masailand, 88
Masai tribe, 60, 99–100
matrix, 93
Mau Mau uprising, 13, 102–103
Miocene era, 50, 96–97, 115, 119,
  120
Miriamu, 8–9
"missing link," 58, 61, 69, 98
Mombasa, Kenya, 2–3
mud shave, 12
Muhia, Joshua, 19–20
Mukiri, Heselon, 118
Myers, J. L., 81–82

National Geographic magazine,
  115
National Geographic Society,
  118, 132
National Press Club, 117
Nature, 69
Ndorobo tribe, 19

Neanderthal man, 52, 54–57
Neolithic era, 24, 27, 29, 33
Newsam, Bernard H., 63, 65–67,
  68, 71
Ngai, 13–14, 23
Ngorongoro crater, 88
Nicol, Mary Douglas, *see*
  Leakey, Mary Douglas Nicol
  (wife)
Njonjo, C., 132
Nutcracker man, 106–109, 125
nyenji cia ngoma ("razors of the
  gods"), 62
nyura-nyura ("divine
  thunderbolts"), 64–65

obsidian, in prehistoric tool
  manufacture, 26, 29, 62, 65
Olduvai Gorge
  geological beds of, 8, 91, 93,
    112–113
  see also excavations,
    paleontological, Olduvai
    Gorge
Olorgesailie, Mount, 98, 99
Olorgesailie museum, 99–100
On the Origin of Species, 50
Oswald, Dr. Felix, 92

Paleolithic era, 76, 81
paleontology, history of, 54–61
Pan African Congress of
  Prehistory and Quarternary
  Studies, 101
Paranthrobus robustus, 98, 108,
  118
Payne, Dr. Melvin, 132
Peking man, 69, 97, 109, 118
  see also Homo erectus
Percy Sladen Memorial Trust, 85